"If you are a teen living with depression and ongoing negative internal chatter, this book is for you. It offers simple, straightforward, doable suggestions and practices for taming your internal critic, and moving from feeling down and out to being up and in—in touch with your best self, and engaged in a meaningful, satisfying life."

—**Amy Saltzman, MD**, author of *A Still Quiet Place for Teens*

"This book provides a gentle introduction to mindfulness, weaving the practice through traditional approaches to the treatment of depression for teens."

—**Lisa M. Schab, LCSW**, psychotherapist and author of *The Self-Esteem Workbook for Teens*, *The Anxiety Workbook for Teens*, and *Beyond the Blues*

"This wonderful book is the voice of a wise and caring friend. This friend believes in you, knows your strengths, and can support and guide you to free yourself from the weight of depression, and experience the joys of life again."

—**Dzung X. Vo, MD**, FAAP, author of *The Mindful Teen*

"Using down-to-earth language and engaging, adolescent-friendly exercises, Mitch Abblett and Christopher Willard draw on their extensive clinical experience to present a comprehensive array of techniques that address the particular challenges of depression. One key feature that sets this book apart from other workbooks on depression is the authors' infusion of mindfulness and positive psychology throughout. Threaded throughout the book is the image of 'Sergeant Mind,' the misguided but powerful inner critic whose influence maintains the depressive state. In its emphasis on the power of the mind, the authors' demystify the characteristics of depression, and help youth move toward a more decentered perspective. This resource, which can be a particularly helpful adjunct to therapy, offers young people body-centered, mental, and interpersonal tools to help them move forward more confidently, capitalize on personal strengths, and act in ways that undercut the power of 'Sgt. Mind.'"

—**Trish Broderick, PhD**, clinical psychologist and research associate at the Bennett Pierce Prevention Research Center at The Pennsylvania State University, author of *Learning to Breathe*, and coauthor of *The Life Span*

"Want to take charge of your own life and improve your mood? Pick up *Mindfulness for Teen Depression*. It offers realistic, accessible ways to feel less overwhelmed and down on yourself and more confident and at ease. Mitch Abblett and Christopher Willard have once again created an easy-to-read book that sets things out in straight-forward fashion. I imagine anyone, not only teens, will find *Mindfulness for Teen Depression* both useful and inspiring."

—**Mark Bertin, MD**, author of *Mindful Parenting for ADHD*

# mindfulness for teen depression

## a workbook for improving your mood

MITCH R. ABBLETT, PhD
CHRISTOPHER WILLARD, PsyD

Instant Help Books
An Imprint of New Harbinger Publications, Inc.

## Publisher's Note

*This publication is designed to provide accurate and authoritative information in regard to the subject matter covered. It is sold with the understanding that the publisher is not engaged in rendering psychological, financial, legal, or other professional services. If expert assistance or counseling is needed, the services of a competent professional should be sought.*

Distributed in Canada by Raincoast Books

Copyright © 2016 by Mitch R. Abblett and Christopher Willard
        Instant Help Books
        An Imprint of New Harbinger Publications, Inc.
        5674 Shattuck Avenue
        Oakland, CA 94609
        www.newharbinger.com

The "Emotional Eating vs. Healthy Eating" chart in chapter 3 of this book is modified from CONSTANT CRAVING A–Z by Doreen Virtue, copyright © 1999 Doreen Virtue. Used by permission of Hay House, Inc., in Carlsbad, CA.

"Floating Leaves on a Moving Stream" is adapted from GET OUT OF YOUR MIND AND INTO YOUR LIFE by Steven C. Hayes and Spencer Smith, copyright © 2005 Steven C. Hayes and Spencer Smith. Used by permission of New Harbinger Publications.

Cover design by Amy Shoup; Acquired by Jess O'Brien; Edited by Karen Schader

### Library of Congress Cataloging-in-Publication Data

Names: Abblett, Mitch, author. | Willard, Christopher (Psychologist), author.
Title: Mindfulness for teen depression : a workbook for improving your mood /
    Mitch R. Abblett and Christopher Willard.
Description: Oakland, CA : New Harbinger Publications, Inc., [2016]
Identifiers: LCCN 2015048183| ISBN 9781626253827 (paperback) | ISBN 9781626253834 (pdf e-book) |
    ISBN 9781626253841 (epub)
Subjects: LCSH: Depression in adolescence--Juvenile literature. | Mindfulness-based cognitive therapy--Juvenile
    literature. | Mindfulness (Psychology)--Juvenile literature. | Depression, Mental--Treatment--Juvenile literature.
    | BISAC: JUVENILE NONFICTION / Social Issues / Depression & Mental Illness. | JUVENILE
    NONFICTION / Social Issues / Emotions & Feelings. | JUVENILE NONFICTION / Social Issues / Friendship.
Classification: LCC RJ506.D4 A23 2016 | DDC 616.85/2700835--dc23 LC record available at http://lccn.loc.
    gov/2015048183

Printed in the United States of America

18    17    16

10   9   8   7   6   5   4   3   2   1               First printing

To all my teen clients over the years: some may have judged you by what you've done or not done on the surface, but you and I know there was always much more to you than that.

—MRA

To young people (and everyone who loves them) everywhere. Especially all of you whom I've known as my patients, my students, and most importantly, my teachers.

—CTW

# Contents

# Introduction

This book was born in a coffee shop. Two psychologists and writers sat together and talked about how they might make a contribution to the mental health of kids and their families. Both had worked for a number of years as therapists with a wide range of children, teens, and their parents; many of these kids were struggling with depression. And both had a passion for the ways positive approaches, such as mindfulness-based interventions, can help people.

So we decided to write it all down. And as we wrote, we realized that the chapters pretty much read the way we talked and worked with our teen clients—direct, authentic, skills focused, and as compassionate and human as possible. What's more, we were, and still are, both devoted to our own personal mindfulness and meditation practices. And so that's what readers—teens like you—will get here in these pages: the straightforward voices of authors who practice what we teach.

It is our clinical experience (and science backs it up) that approaches based in mindfulness and positive psychology are effective in helping people manage and move through the struggles of depression. The skills offered here are all about building your powers of awareness to see yourself and what's around you more clearly, and to be less bogged down in painful emotions and self-defeating habits. This book is about learning to open up what depression has closed down.

The time is right for this particular book. Take a look at the following statistics:

- In 2014, researchers found that young adults who had been clinically depressed during their teen years were more likely to *ruminate*, which means to get stuck in repeating their thoughts over and over.

- A study published in 2014 suggests that teen girls' greater exposure to stressful peer interactions may lead to more rumination and more risk of depression.

- About 11 percent of adolescents have a depressive disorder by age eighteen. That's two or three kids in every classroom and on every soccer team, and dozens (if not hundreds) in your school alone.

- According to the World Health Organization, major depressive disorder is the leading cause of disability among Americans from ages fifteen to forty-four.

On the positive side, let's also look at the following:

- In a 2013 study of about four hundred adolescent students, a mindfulness-based program significantly reduced teens' reports of depressive symptoms, and this was still the case at a six-month follow-up.

- A team of scientists has shown that simply expecting to be happy about something actually leads to neurochemical changes in the brain that immediately make you happier.

- New research suggests that exercise may not only help manage someone's existing depression but also actually help protect the mind against future depression.

So yes, the time is right for you to be picking up this workbook. Depression is unfortunately too common for thousands of teens these days. But it's also becoming increasingly common for therapists and people in general to learn and apply positive approaches such as mindfulness (which we'll define for you shortly) to assist with many things in life, even the darkness of depression.

# How to Use This Book

Although we've designed this book as a workbook, we hope it doesn't feel like work. We want it to be informative, helpful, and maybe even fun. Our goal is for you to interact with the material and come away with skills that not only work for you but that you'll also find useful enough to actually do.

One thing is certain—you'll get out of this book only what you're willing to put into it. Giving the exercises, activities, and strategies a shot is very important, and even if some feel lame or like a lot of work, we encourage you to try anyway. This is *not* a book to be read passively. It needs your attention and active effort. The book offers various activities, meditations, and questions for you to consider. We recommend that you pause at each, give it a thoughtful try, and move on only when you're ready. You don't have to write everything down in the spaces provided, but at least spend a few moments reflecting internally. Some of the materials can be downloaded at http://www.newharbinger.com/33827; you'll find instructions at the back of the book for accessing these materials.

We recommend going through the pages in order (because the skills build on each other), but you can also try out various things from different chapters. All the skills complement and support each other. We definitely encourage you to go back again and again to anything that works for you, even if it works only a bit. At the end of each chapter, you will find a section titled "Down and Out or Up and In?" which is your chance to put into action in the coming days the skills you learned in that chapter. It's your chance to decide what wins out—being in a down mood and feeling left out of the flow of your life, or using skills we're suggesting to bring your mood up and leaning in toward engaging in daily life.

# Decisions, Decisions: How This Book Will Help

We live in a world where we are bombarded by choices about everything, including how to deal with depression. TV ads may suggest one medication, your parents may tell you to get more sleep, your friends may suggest yoga—and that's all before you even talk to a professional! You might feel like you understand depression a bit but still be at something of a loss about what to actually do about it.

This book will help you sort through those choices to find what works best for you and your depression, and we suggest you figure that out with the help and support of someone else. Feedback and positive support are helpful for building a new skill and are crucial for managing depression, so push yourself to share your experience of the activities and your responses with someone who feels safe: a therapist or counselor if you have one, or perhaps a parent, mentor, trusted friend, or even a group. That decision alone will make a huge difference.

One thing we do think is important: whatever you do, commit to sticking with it for a while!

# chapter 1

# A New View of Depression

Nothing can bring you peace but yourself.

—Ralph Waldo Emerson

Nothing any book or therapist could ever say could possibly do justice to the reality of depression. There's just no way to say it lightly. Depression sucks.

When you're depressed, everything—the universe, the future, your own self—can look hopeless and bleak. It may look like a dark world out there, but in this book, and in your life, you're the hero. We, the authors, view depression as the struggle you're up against, and we're here to help you rewrite your own story. In this chapter, we help you understand your depression with more information on what it is and what it can feel like.

Before we dive in with a closer look at definitions of depression and mindfulness, and before you start learning and practicing new skills, we'd like to have you do a brief visualization activity.

## Try This: Visualization

Sit quietly in a place where you won't be disturbed for a few minutes. Imagine that you're out hiking in the woods on a beautiful day. You've got a large pack strapped to your back, the air is crisp, the tree branches around you are swaying in the breeze, and birds are singing. You're feeling good and are glad you decided to head out into the wild.

You're so busy checking out the scenery that you don't notice a huge, gaping sinkhole in front of you, and you suddenly topple down into it. Before you can do anything, you've rolled all the way to the bottom and are lying flat on your back. You're not hurt, but you're a bit freaked out—this hole is very deep, and the sides are incredibly steep. You try frantically, but there's no climbing out. You call for help, but you're so far out in the middle of nowhere that it could be days before someone comes by.

What are you going to do to get out of the hole? You open your pack and find a small shovel. It's the only tool you have, so you start digging. As you dig, you're getting more frustrated and upset. All you have is the shovel, so you keep digging.

What's happening to the hole you're in? Well, if you're digging, it's just going to get deeper! Why would you keep using the shovel when all it's doing is making the hole bigger, trapping you even more?

Here's the thing—when people are depressed, it can feel sort of like they're in a big hole like this. You can feel stuck, even trapped by the symptoms. Through no fault of your own, you fell into this hole of depression, and you've been doing the best you can to dig your way out (we firmly believe this!) with the tools you've had available to you. You've been using different "shovels" (maybe how you use your emotions with others to get their attention, or staying in bed, or perhaps eating too much or too little, or avoiding certain situations). Whatever these tools are, you've used them to try to take care of yourself, to lessen the weight of depression for yourself.

In the space below, jot down a few of the tools you've already tried to get out of the stuck place you've been in, tools that maybe aren't getting you out of the hole:

_____

_____

_____

And here are the questions: Are the tools you've been using working? Are they digging you deeper or are they getting you out? If not, are you willing to learn some new tools? Are you willing to try getting out of the hole in completely new ways? If so, read on.

# Sergeant Mind

Depression is ordered around, and made worse, by an out-of-control inner critic we like to refer to as Sergeant Mind. For simplicity's sake (and because we're both guys and tend to visualize our own "sergeants" that way), we're calling Sgt. Mind a "he," but if "she" fits better for you, by all means visualize the good sergeant that way.

The sergeant is the aspect of your mind—your thoughts and mental images—whispering criticism and negativity in your ear. He tries to keep your world small so that you don't feel overwhelmed or like a failure. But as he tries to protect you by holding the rest of the world at a distance, he's like a stern and overprotective parent who also keeps you isolated, feeling unworthy, and hesitant to take action and make changes.

He's highly skilled and experienced at what he does. When he shows up barking out negative, critical, and gloomy thoughts that can make your depression worse, he's pretty confident that he's right. He also thinks he's pretty smart, but he's spent so much time planning and controlling things from inside his bunker that his view of the world is narrow and distorted.

We all have a Sgt. Mind, an inner critic; it's just that when we experience depression, this critic has been promoted because of all his success in taking control of things. His voice is louder, more insistent, and more believable. It doesn't mean that you're broken or crazy, or that Sgt. Mind is evil and needs to be defeated. Believe it or not, he's trying to help, but he's just confused and misguided. He's stuck viewing the world from behind his dark-colored field glasses, seeing danger around every corner, and is trying to protect you by keeping you from doing anything differently. It probably works in the short run, but the problem is that he makes things worse for you in the long run. We want to help you work with him and turn him into a supportive ally by the end of this book.

Sgt. Mind may look and sound a little different for everyone. Sometimes his voice has echoes of other people in your life—family, teachers, other kids, or voices from the media.

If you were to describe what your own Sgt. Mind looks and sounds like, how would you do so? While it might seem a little silly, it can be very helpful to start practicing the skill of separating the depressive thoughts, emotions, and actions from who you are at your core: the "you" who wants a life that feels good and is going somewhere important.

Who is Sgt. Mind for you?

_____

_____

_____

What does your sergeant look like?

_____

_____

_____

_____

_____

What sort of tone does Sgt. Mind use with you?

_____

_____

Does his voice ever sound like other voices you hear in your life?

_____

_____

What sorts of things does he say about you?

_____

_____

_____

About others?

_____

_____

_____

About the world?

_____

_____

_____

About your future?

_____

_____

_____

# What Is Depression?

Depression is often viewed as a disease, or a condition people have. We believe, and research backs us up on this, that depression is not something you "have" but something you sometimes experience—biologically, mentally, emotionally, socially, and in your behavior. It's not what you are or will be all the time, just like you won't always be a teenager, a student, or (thankfully!) someone living in your parents' house.

Sgt. Mind wears his dark-colored glasses, and because of them, everything he sees is dark, blurry, and distorted. It's the same with depression; it's not you that's the problem, but instead it's the "dark glasses" that put a dark, drab, and negative filter over the world, yourself, and others.

We're not saying that the pain of depression isn't real—it absolutely is. It's just that you're in a much better place to manage and overcome depression if you can find ways to clear the glasses that make everything look so…depressing. A main goal for this book is to provide you with new, empowering skills for directly facing and managing depression, by seeing what is the depression's view, and what is the reality of your life.

# The Diagnosis of Depression

We all feel down from time to time, especially when we experience sad, traumatic, or stressful things. But if we continue to feel down or have a lot of these symptoms for more than a few weeks, it could mean depression.

Below are some symptoms of clinical depression. If you're experiencing even a few of these for more than a few weeks, check in with your doctor, therapist, or another trusted adult. Some symptoms might have a cause that isn't depression, so it's very important to check in with a medical professional and have a physical exam before you or someone else decides you are experiencing depression.

Read over this list and write down your thoughts about each group of symptoms. It's unlikely you'll have much to say about many of them, but you may have a lot to say about a few of them.

### Bodily and physical symptoms

- Aches, pains, cramps, and digestive problems that don't respond to the usual treatment

  *Have you noticed more physical discomforts or medical problems like these recently?*

- Feeling exhausted or having much less energy

  *Do things seem to take more energy than they used to? Have you been feeling tired or sluggish?*

- Overeating or undereating with 5 percent weight gain or loss

  *Have you found yourself eating a lot mindlessly to cope? Or losing your appetite altogether?*

- Insomnia, disrupted sleeping, or too much sleeping

  *Are you over- or undersleeping (and not just because of homework, or staying up late texting or playing video games)? Are you having more trouble falling asleep or staying asleep?*

- Psychomotor changes

  *Is your body more agitated and fidgety than usual? Or do you find yourself moving more slowly than usual? Have other people noticed this?*

_____

_____

_____

_____

### Psychological symptoms

- Feeling guilty when you don't need to, feeling like a bad person

  *Are you feeling unnecessarily guilty about things that aren't such a big deal? Have your self-esteem and self-worth been crashing?*

- Feeling hopeless or pessimistic

  *Have things been feeling pointless or hopeless? Are you struggling to see the positive or noticing that a lot of things seem negative? Do you feel like your attitude toward life has changed for the worse?*

- Sad, empty, depressed, or anxious feelings

  *Are you feeling sad more often? Do you feel empty, hollow, or numb inside? Are you crying more often and not sure why?*

- Thoughts of death, thoughts of suicide, suicide attempts

  *Have you been thinking about suicide or death more than usual?*

  _____

  _____

  _____

  _____

### Social and behavioral symptoms

- Loss of interest in your usual activities and interests

  *Do your favorite things (for example, friends, activities, TV shows) not interest you as much? Is your sex drive lower than usual?*

- Irritability, restlessness

  *Do little things annoy you more than usual? Are you getting bored more quickly?*

  _____

  _____

  _____

  _____

Do any of these symptoms look familiar to you? Which ones most jumped out at you? Did any of them surprise you?

_____

_____

_____

_____

_____

_____

# You're Not Alone

You might wonder, *Why me?* It might actually be helpful to ask, *Why not me?* Because about one in four people will experience a mood disorder at some point in their lives, we believe you might be better off learning to manage depression while you're young, to get the skills you need to last a lifetime.

Have you ever wondered what you have in common with at least three US presidents, as well as Britney Spears, Beyoncé, and Buzz Aldrin, the second man on the moon? Okay, probably not—but what you have in common is that you've all experienced difficulty with depression.

There are literally millions of successful people walking around in the world who have experienced depression, come out the other side of it stronger, and gone on to do incredible things. Here is a partial list of other folks who have wrestled with their own Sgt. Mind, according to interviews and historical research:

- Artists Henri Matisse, Jackson Pollock, and Mark Rothko

- Authors Stephen King and J. K. Rowling

- Award-winning actors Christian Bale, Jim Carrey, Harrison Ford, Angelina Jolie, and Gwyneth Paltrow

- Award-winning musicians Janet Jackson and Anthony Kiedis

- Billionaire businessman Ted Turner

- Classical composers Wolfgang Mozart and Ludwig van Beethoven

- Physicist Sir Isaac Newton

- Pro basketball players Delonte West and Jerry West

- Rappers André 3000, Eminem, and Kendrick Lamar

- Talk-show hosts and comedians Ellen DeGeneres and Rosie O'Donnell

- US presidents Abraham Lincoln, John Adams, and Calvin Coolidge

And remember, this is only a partial list of well-known successful people. Just think of all the other people in your school; it could be dozens, if not hundreds, of kids in your school, at your camp, and on your teams. If you're interested, just type in something like "athletes with depression" (or "musicians" or "entrepreneurs") into a search engine and see who comes up. We can almost guarantee you will find a role model who's been through this.

Sgt. Mind likes to tell you that you're alone, and that depression will keep you from living a full life. We're here to tell you otherwise; the good news is that depression is treatable, and the vast majority of people with depression get better!

# The Bio-Psycho-Social Model

Hopefully this section will help you understand that the "why" of depression is not as simple as saying "It's in my genes," "It's a chemical imbalance," or "My family and I have been through a lot." All of those may be true and may be contributing factors. But in the end, this book is not as much about why you're depressed, but rather what you do about it on a daily basis that will help you feel better.

Research is clear that many people who struggle with some forms of depression may have biological factors, such as genetics or medical issues, that contribute to the problem. But the research is also clear that it's not as simple as inheriting a few bummer DNA strands.

In the past, people believed all kinds of things about what caused intense negative emotions, from demons to the alignment of the stars. More recently, debate has raged as to whether it is totally biological or totally based on childhood experiences—nature or nurture. Nowadays, experts believe that our emotional issues are rooted in what they call the *bio-psycho-social model*. This fancy-sounding term means that biology is one factor, but we also consider what's happening in people's thoughts and emotions (psychology) as well as their social relationships and situations (behavior). We think about the way these all interact to contribute to depression. But just as factors like biology, thought patterns, and social experiences can contribute to your depression, they can also contribute to your recovery.

We've designed this book around this model because the science is clear that working with your body, your mind, and your relationships and behavior is most likely to lead to powerful results. We've included a chapter on each to help you and your support team design an approach to your life that gives you clear and effective tools for each one. They all fit together in moving forward when Sgt. Mind would have you giving up.

# Depression Has Many Faces

Depression is not simply crying or feeling sad all the time. In fact, for teens, depression can look very different. There are many symptoms of depression besides sadness. For the most part, they reflect feelings of withdrawal and loss of interest in life.

People often don't recognize depression because it doesn't look how it looks on TV or how others in the culture describe it. For that reason, we've included a list of some of the words we've heard both kids and adults use to describe depression. Look it over, and circle whichever ones you identify with.

**Physical**

| | |
|---|---|
| Agitated | Hollow |
| Bleak | Languishing |
| Constant lump in the throat | Lethargic |
| Crushed | Lifeless |
| Dead inside | Listless |
| Debilitated | Numb |
| Deflated | Oppressed |
| Dull | Stranded |
| Empty | Stuck |
| Exhausted | Trapped |
| Fatigued | Vacant |
| Feeling underwater | Weak |
| Heavy | |

## Psychological

Absent

Adrift

Aimless

Alone

Anguished

Apathetic

Ashamed

Bereft

Bitter

Blank

Bored

Broken

Cloudy

Defeated

Defective

Desolate

Despondent

Detached

Disconnected

Disengaged

Disinterested

Dissociated

Drab

Emotionless

Endless blackness

Foggy

Frustrated

Futile

Grief without cause

Guilty

Hazy

Helpless

Hopeless

In a black hole

Irritable

Irritated

Joyless

Lacking

Lackluster

Like everyone
hates me

Lonely

Lost

Meaningless

Melancholy

Misery

Not there

On the outside
looking in

Painful

Pointless

Purposeless

Remorseful

Self-hating

Self-loathing

Unfulfilled

Ungrounded

Unloved

Unwanted

Zombie-like

This isn't the SAT, and you may not recognize every word or phrase on this list or relate to them. The bad news is they're all painful to hear, and even more painful to live with. The good news is that no matter what you've circled on the list, you're not alone. Others—people we authors know, in fact—have had those feelings and gone on to feel better.

Which words jumped out at you the most?

_____

_____

What words or phrases might you add?

_____

_____

_____

_____

Is there a pattern to the kinds of words and phrases you related to? If so, what is it?

_____

_____

_____

Who do you feel safe sharing this list with? If no one comes to mind, don't worry—we'll help you figure this out in chapter 5.

_____

_____

_____

_____

# Depression in Disguise

Depression has a tendency to disguise itself and can look invisible on the outside. In fact, it can even be invisible from the inside. Here are stories of three young people who may not have looked obviously depressed from the outside or even realized they were depressed.

Kara looked like she had it all. Everyone knew her as the popular and pretty girl, the girl with varsity letters in field hockey, and on the honor roll. She held it together so well in school and made it look so easy online, but the mask fell off in her therapist's office. Even though she seemed to have it together, she felt like it was all going to fall apart. The pressure she was putting on herself was pushing her deeper into depression.

She didn't cry in public, and only twice did she cry in a therapy session. Once it was over a breakup, and once over the loss of her grandmother. She had very little appetite and walked around with an upset stomach most days. Even when she got her homework done at a reasonable hour, she struggled to fall asleep and woke up early, before she was fully rested. She was constantly on edge. It all looked so good on the outside, but on the inside, she felt undeserving of all her success.

Kara had physical symptoms like lack of appetite, stomachaches, and difficulty sleeping. She also felt restless and agitated a lot of the time, with an increasingly pessimistic attitude toward life. Kara didn't isolate herself or show any other warning signs from the outside, but nevertheless, according to the symptoms, Kara was depressed.

Did you relate to any aspects of Kara's story or the ways symptoms appeared for her? If so, which ones?

_____

_____

_____

_____

Lucas was restless, irritable, and discontented. Like a lot of young men his age, his depression didn't manifest as sadness, but rather as disinterest in school, which turned into frustration with himself, which in turn he took out on everyone around him. He put on about fifteen pounds over the fall term, which only made him feel worse about himself. He started staying home more on weekends, when he would sleep in until noon and then stay in bed for the rest of the day.

His mother brought him to therapy for help with school, not for depression. Lucas wasn't performing up to his potential—or at least that's what his teachers and family thought. He did tell his therapist that school hadn't been going as well as it used to, that focusing was harder, and that he forgot details on his assignments more often. His lacrosse coach was telling him he had "lost his hustle," and he did feel clumsier when he was playing. Lucas also used to love science, but that changed this year, even though he had the same teacher he had loved last year.

Lucas had symptoms like lack of concentration and disinterest in his favorite subjects. He was irritable and grumpy, gaining weight, losing coordination a bit, and withdrawing from friends. Lucas had more than enough symptoms to qualify for depression even though he never exactly felt sad.

Did you relate to any aspects of Lucas's story or the ways symptoms appeared for him? If so, which ones?

_____

_____

_____

_____

Vanessa was "high school famous." If it were time for yearbook superlatives, she'd probably get voted class clown—she was always the first to make silly comments out of nowhere and at all the wrong times in classes. She seemed to live in detention but no longer appeared bothered by getting in trouble. She was often late to class or wandering the halls, and if someone was making noise out in the hall during class, it was a good bet it was Vanessa.

Though everyone knew who Vanessa was, no one seemed to know much about her. She was loud, but also a loner. She kept mostly to herself and never participated in clubs, sports, or any social gatherings outside of school.

What they definitely didn't know was that she was struggling with suicidal thoughts and impulses, scratching and cutting herself to manage her sadness and lonely feelings, and sleeping much more than usual for someone her age.

When kids began posting nasty rumors that were obviously not true about her, her parents and administrators at school got involved. Vanessa wasn't in school for a while after that.

Vanessa might have been silly and clowning a lot, but her smile was a thin covering over her depression. Even though she was not acting or looking sad in public, no one at school was seeing what people in her family and the treatment professionals who worked with her outside of school knew.

Did you relate to any aspects of Vanessa's story or the ways symptoms appeared for her? Which ones?

_____

_____

_____

_____

# Envisioning a World Without Depression

When we are in the depths of a depression, it can be hard to see out of it, or remember what it's like to not be depressed. Sgt. Mind shows us only the worst-case scenarios and tends to hide other perspectives on life. It can help to hold in mind what the opposite of that negativity is, for those low moments. Ask yourself the following questions, and jot down any answers that come to you.

How would you feel about yourself if you weren't depressed? Or even if you were a bit less depressed?

_____

_____

_____

How would you feel about the future if you weren't depressed? Or even if you were a bit less depressed?

_____

_____

_____

What would be in that future? What things would you have and be doing, and who would you be doing them with?

_____

_____

_____

_____

_____

How will you feel about the world and about other people when you aren't depressed?

_____

_____

_____

# A Word on Suicide and Self-Harm

Sometimes things get so bad that, like Vanessa, people think about hurting or even killing themselves, or just don't care about being alive. If you ever feel that way, it is important that you have adults you trust whom you can speak to. In chapter 5, you'll have an opportunity to write out a list of support people you feel comfortable speaking to in tough times.

Because this is a book and not an actual interaction, we obviously can't be there to talk you through any thoughts of suicide or self-harm. We can't emphasize enough how important it is for you to talk with others, even if it feels pointless and no matter what Sgt. Mind might be telling you. Any of those reactions are normal, _and_ they're part of depression. But if you feel like hurting yourself or ending your life, you absolutely must talk to an adult because they can really help and keep you safe.

With that, we'd like you to be willing to make a commitment right now to talking with your therapist about creating an agreement or "safety contract." This agreement will be between you, your therapist, and perhaps other important people in your life, and will be all about committing to keeping yourself safe by reaching out when things are getting especially dangerous. Though Sgt. Mind might make fun of this idea, once you're free and clear of depression, you'll be glad you did it.

# A Word on Medication

For some people, one part of depression treatment, besides the exercises in this workbook and talking to your therapist, might be medication. Medication won't fix everything, but it may help you get to a point where talk therapy can work better, and it may lend you the strength to do the practices in this workbook or the hard work of talk therapy. Medication isn't for everyone, but it might be helpful for you. You, your family, and your therapist, doctor, or nurse can decide together what makes the most sense for your particular depression.

If you're taking medication, there are a few important things to consider. Ask your prescriber about potential side effects, and be sure to let an adult know if you experience any. One thing to remember about medication (or talk therapy, or workbooks) is that it doesn't always work right away, and some days will still be better than others. Medication usually takes a few weeks to kick in, and longer than that before it starts working best.

The important thing is that you take your medication regularly and as prescribed, not changing or missing any doses, even when you start to feel better.

# Sgt. Mind's Best Lines and Worst Lies

Sgt. Mind is very likely to be throwing misunderstandings your way. The myths below are things Sgt. Mind would have you believe about yourself and depression. Do any sound familiar to you?

- "Depression is my fault."

- "Depression is someone else's fault."

- "Depression will prevent me from having a good life or the life I want."

- "Depression means I'm broken."

- "Depression means I'll always need medication or therapy."

- "Depression means I'm the mental kid (or the special ed kid or therapy kid)."

- "Depression means I'll never measure up."

- "Depression means my parents will treat me like a baby."

Sgt. Mind's lines may seem accurate, but check in with other people and your own authentic experience about whether they are really as true as they sound.

# Making Sense of Different Mood Disorders

Depression can be experienced in many ways on its own or as part of other issues. As graduate students in psychology, we sat in endless lectures and read countless books to understand all the various psychological issues people struggle with. Summarizing those hours we spent learning about depression, it is important for you to understand these facts:

- Not all mood disorders and depressions are the same.

- Some will respond better to some treatments than others.

- Because depression has many symptoms, and because every person is unique, depression can look (and feel) different for different people.

- You're not alone. More than one teen in ten will experience depression before age eighteen, and up to one in four will experience it at some point in their lifetimes.

Here are a few short descriptions of depression-related conditions that commonly affect teens like you and your classmates, teammates, and friends.

- *Major depression:* For those with major depression, their low moods can affect many things, including concentration; feeling good about themselves, others, and the future; and withdrawing from relationships and activities. Major depression is more than just a "down day" or the "blues" and needs to be diagnosed and treated by a professional. When it is severe, there are risks of considering self-harm or suicide. Both medicines and talk therapy are effective, as well as making changes in your life, and especially all of these together. The mindfulness and other practices in this book have been selected to be effective with major depression.

- *Dysthymia:* This is basically a less intense but more long-term version of major depression. The symptoms are not as severe but still get in the way of daily functioning. For teens, significant irritability is often a telltale symptom. Of course, there is a lot to be irritable about as a teen, so again, it is important to get a diagnosis from a professional.

- *Bipolar disorder:* People with this disorder experience major mood swings over time between periods of depressed mood and periods of dangerously high mood. In the highs, they may take unnecessary risks beyond the average teenager, and daily life is disrupted to the point that it becomes very hard to function in school or relationships. These are not just ordinary mood swings and need to be diagnosed by a professional who knows the person very well.

The main differences between these mood disorders are the ways mood changes, the intensity of these changes, and how long the changes last. All of us experience changes in our moods every day, but for people diagnosed with one of these types of disorders, the mood changes and intensity are getting in the way of school and relationships. And they have to be diagnosed by a mental health professional, not themselves, a parent, a friend, or a teacher. There are a few other things that can affect moods, such as hormones, seasons, substances, sleep, and nutrition, as well as other medical conditions, so a physical exam is essential.

# Shifting Your Perspective

Close this book for a moment, and take a look at the word "depression" on the cover. Really look at it; in fact, put it right up to your eyeball. How much can you really see of the world when depression is in your face like this?

Now slowly move your hands away, so that you can see the word and the cover, then back farther so that you can see the whole room, and the text is just a small part of your view.

That's how we want to change your relationship to depression—not to pretend it isn't there, but to make it smaller and yourself bigger so that it doesn't block out everything you see, especially when it blocks seeing what's actually going well.

Instead of telling yourself that you're depressed, try to shift toward a stance of having thoughts. Try saying to yourself, *I'm having the thought that I'm depressed.* Or even, *Depression is visiting.* How does this sound compared to saying that you're depressed? This attitude creates a small space between the thought and you, in order for choice and possibilities to occur.

You can also think, *Sgt. Mind is telling me that the world is a terrible place, that I'm terrible, and nothing will ever work out.* What happens to your experience of Sgt. Mind–like negative thoughts about depression when you shift them like this? Are they as intense as usual, or do they ease a bit?

Sgt. Mind wants you alone, disconnected from your body and mind, looking at yourself, the world, and the future with the dark glasses of negativity. He does so because he wants to keep your world small and safe. He'll tell you all his negative, critical things through sensations and physical reactions in your body, in your thoughts and mental images, and in what you do (and don't do) in your interactions with others. That's why the bio-psycho-social approach is important: it gets at all the places where Sgt. Mind has an unhelpful influence, and helps turn things around.

In this book, you will learn how mindfulness—the open-eyed opposite of Sgt. Mind—can help you see things clearly, connect with others, link up your body and mind to function as a unit, and go after what matters to you now, in the present moment.

Sgt. Mind plays it safe and traps you in suffering. Mindfulness and positive psychology may feel risky at times, but when you open up, the suffering tends to fade. Which feels more doable to you?

# Unearthing the Positives

We want to end this, well, depressing chapter about depression on a high note. One big part of this book is positive psychology: the idea that our strengths are just as important as our so-called weaknesses. They are certainly more important in helping you work with your depression.

You'll look more closely at your strengths in chapter 4. For now, imagine you're brainstorming a book about your life, written many years from now as you look back at what got you through the hard times and made you stronger. Consider these questions as you come up with ideas.

What is your greatest strength?

_____

_____

What is one hard thing you have overcome?

_____

_____

What helped you through that hard time in the past?

_____

_____

What is one thing others admire about you?

_____

_____

What words of wisdom would you offer a struggling friend or sibling?

_____

_____

_____

_____

Pick at least one role model who has overcome adversity. Why do you admire that person?

_____

_____

_____

What is at least one important positive event that has shaped you into the person that you are?

_____

_____

Which people can you rely on who have had or continue to have a positive impact on you? (Consider teachers, friends, classmates, teammates, coaches, family, clergy, counselors, and others.)

_____

_____

_____

_____

_____

What inspirational quotes, poems, and songs have gotten you through hard times in the past? Can you put one on your mirror, or make it the background of your phone or computer?

_____

_____

_____

_____

_____

_____

Remember, this is *your* life, *your* story. No matter what Sgt. Mind tells you, don't write a story that leaves out all the effort you've put into taking care of yourself.

# Down and Out or Up and In?

In this chapter, we offered some basic definitions of depression and explored some of the ways it can manifest in different people. As you finish up the chapter, you may still hear Sgt. Mind barking orders and expressing doubt. If not, great; if so, don't worry—you'll learn to manage him in the coming chapters.

What have you learned from this chapter about how depression gets you *down* in your mood so that you're checking *out* of daily life?

_____

_____

_____

_____

What specific strategies or ideas from this chapter might help you lift your mood *up* and move you *in* toward people and activities?

_____

_____

_____

_____

What one strategy, idea, or tool are you willing to put to use in the next twenty-four hours? Write it here, and commit to doing so.

_____

_____

_____

# chapter 2

# A Closer Look at Mindfulness and Positive Psychology

Life moves pretty fast. If you don't stop and look around once in a while, you could miss it.

—Ferris Bueller

The word "mindfulness" seems to be everywhere these days. You may have even heard it before you picked up (or were handed) this book. And while you probably have a sense of what it is (because you've already experienced it), you'll get the most from this book if we start this chapter with a definition that feels clear to you.

"Positive psychology" may be less familiar to you. We want to clarify that it's much more than just finding silver linings, or skipping about in search of unicorns and rainbows. As we'll see in the second part of this chapter, positive psychology is about down-to-earth, practical, scientific exercises for health, well-being, and happiness.

Both mindfulness and positive psychology help you manage depression. Mindfulness helps you manage your attention, and positive psychology gives you concrete tools for shaping your outlook and actions. This chapter will help you understand how, together, they make for powerful allies against depression.

# What Is Mindfulness?

We define *mindfulness* like this: paying attention…to the present moment…with acceptance and without judgment.

This definition has three parts, and we can look at each of them individually, as well as looking at them as a whole.

## Paying Attention

The first thing about mindfulness, and what might have made you cringe if you've ever had someone snap at you to pay attention, is paying attention. To understand what's happening in your experience, even in depression, you need to tune in to what's happening and get good information about your depression, rather than turn away from it. Scary, we know. To work with Sgt Mind and your depression, you need to pay attention to what it's telling you, and how it's telling you that—the signals it's sending to your body and mind, and the way it's influencing your behavior.

## The Present Moment

The idea of the present moment is not as new-agey as it might sound. Being in the present is really an opportunity to let go of the past, whether it's thinking about scary or sad things, or just something dumb you said at a party. It's also letting go of the worries about the future, whether it's a prom date, the SATs, or the fate of the planet. In the present moment, you can just relax. The present moment also doesn't last very long, and it's the only time where you actually have any power to do anything. One other surprising fact from research in mindfulness and positive psychology is that what you're doing matters less to your happiness than how much you're paying attention to what you're doing.

You don't have to sit on a cushion or move to a mountaintop to practice mindfulness. You can practice mindfulness informally, just bringing present-moment awareness to anything or everything you do, which will in turn boost your happiness. All the things you already do on a daily basis—eating, hygiene, chores, walking, arts, performing, practicing, studying—can be done mindfully.

## With Acceptance and Without Judgment

Some people say "with kindness and curiosity" instead. This part of the definition is a little trickier, and it asks for a different relationship than we tend to have to our thoughts and our experience. Usually, we are judging ourselves, our thoughts, and the world around us harshly. With mindfulness, we are trying to stay away from that. Whether struggling with depression or not, many of us hear Sgt. Mind telling us:

- "I'm not good enough."

- "People are going to think less of me."

- "I'm failing and should just give up."

- "Others will let me down."

- "There's something just fundamentally wrong with me."

- "I'm weird, and I'll always be an outsider."

- "I'm unlovable."

- "I'll never accomplish anything."

A lot of people, maybe even most people, including successful adults, struggle with self-judging thoughts like these. This is where nonjudgment of the thoughts can be so helpful, because it also means that you don't have to believe everything you think, and it helps you realize that feelings aren't facts. Those ideas may both sound strange at first, but hopefully over the course of this book they will start to make sense. Sgt. Mind tells you that what he thinks is true and that what you feel is always true. In fact, sometimes our thoughts and feelings are accurate, sometimes not. With mindfulness, we can see which ones are worth paying attention to, and which ones we can let go of. Carl Rogers, a famous psychologist, writes: "The curious thing is, when I accept myself exactly as I am, then I can change."

The word "acceptance" is tricky. You may have thought of it as being about liking something. Here, we aren't asking you to like your experience, just to notice it and try not to fight with it in this moment. If you fight the thought, it will stick around even more, like if we asked you to not think about a pink elephant. On the other hand, trying to hold on to positive thoughts or moods is also hard; if we asked you to only think about pink elephants, your mind would wander off soon enough. Worse, you might feel like more of a failure!

It's also very important to understand that, when we talk about acceptance, we're not saying that you should just suck it up and get used to tough emotions and difficult experiences. Acceptance is about openness and willingness, not stoicism. Rather than Sgt. Mind saying, "I need to get over this or control this," acceptance is about willingness and saying to yourself, *I'm willing to face this and go through it.*

Acceptance, in the mindful sense we're using it, is different because it comes out of an understanding that things *will* change, even if not always on the timeline we want. Sgt. Mind would like us to believe that bad feelings will stick around forever, but check in with your actual experience—are you still having that same exact bad feeling you had when you were in kindergarten? Probably not. Things change. When we watch our experience with mindfulness, we see firsthand that thoughts, feelings, and sensations all come and go.

It's when you can't accept what's happening now, when you try to fight your thoughts, feelings, or behavior, or judge them harshly, that you feel worse about yourself, and exhausted to boot.

# You Probably Already Know Mindfulness

Mindfulness isn't actually about adding something on; in fact, it's about letting go of the stuff that's in the way of our natural, contented state. You've probably already experienced elements of mindfulness in your life, even if you never used that word. This book will help you practice getting back to that mind state over and over again, building a clear path to get there, so you can find it more quickly when you really need it.

## Try This: Connecting with Mindfulness

Let's do a quick visualization. Close your eyes and let your mind settle on a situation where you completely lost track of time. Maybe it was something that was so amazing, so awe-inspiring, engaging, entertaining—something that completely focused and absorbed you. Perhaps it was a sporting event you were participating in. A piece of music you were playing. A conversation with someone that drew you in completely. A moment in nature or with an animal. Whatever it was, let yourself dive into the memory of it—using all your senses to dip yourself back into it as if it were happening all over again.

That is mindfulness: full engagement of your attention in the present moment without judgment. But don't worry too much about the words defining mindfulness. The experiences of mindfulness you've already had are the best definition.

Chris looks back on a few times in life where he felt so connected, even before he'd heard of mindfulness. Gazing into the embers of a fire at night, watching clouds pass by in the summer sky, or listening to the sounds of rain in the forest from the comfort of his tent and sleeping bag.

Mitch thinks of standing on a mountain in Vermont as a young man, a silent moment in childhood gazing out across the open expanse of a yellow cornfield against the blue sky.

And both think of the moments when their children were born.

What are some moments from your past where you have already felt some aspects of mindfulness?

_____

_____

_____

_____

What do these moments have in common for you?

_____

_____

_____

_____

You may not be able to go back to those specific moments, but you can cultivate a path to those feelings, to feel that way more often.

## Try This: Simple Mindfulness Meditation

To practice mindfulness meditation, whether for a few seconds or longer, all you do is rest your mind on something in the present moment, what we call an "anchor." Your body or breath are often good ones, because while our minds are usually racing to the past or future, our bodies and five senses are in the present. Then, when your mind wanders, you notice where it has gone and gently bring it back to where it was. Again, notice that this involves those three parts: attention, present moment, and acceptance with nonjudgment.

- Set a timer for three minutes.

- Find a comfortable, alert posture with your head and back upright and shoulders relaxed. Bring awareness to either your breath or one of your five senses, and just rest it there.

- Pretty soon you'll notice that your mind starts to wander. That's normal; don't worry, or judge yourself.

- When your mind wanders, just notice where it has gone, then gently but firmly guide it back to your anchor and repeat the process.

Congratulations! You've just practiced three minutes of mindfulness meditation.

## What did you notice doing this practice? What surprised you?

_____

_____

_____

_____

## What happened to Sgt. Mind's voice for you? Did it get louder or softer or not change at all?

_____

_____

# How Does Mindfulness Work?

Well, in three ways. By keeping your attention somewhere and bringing it back, you're building the muscle of concentration in your mind and brain. This trains your mind to stay in the present moment and not get carried off by darker thoughts of depression.

By noticing where your mind went, you're starting to know your mind better, to learn its triggers, patterns, and habits. These insights help you prepare for situations that might start an avalanche of depressive thoughts, feelings, and actions.

And by being gentle and kind with yourself when your mind wanders off, you're creating a new habit of being a little nicer to yourself—sometimes called *self-compassion*—which is not something most of us are in the habit of doing, especially when we're depressed. This helps quiet Sgt. Mind.

Some of the practices in this book emphasize awareness, concentration, and attention to the present moment. Others focus on insight, and still others on compassion and self-compassion, all of which are useful at different moments, and all of which can help you manage your depression.

So let's take a moment to think about mindfulness in terms of depression. Once again, the definition of mindfulness: paying attention to the present-moment experience with acceptance and without judgment. And what would you say is the opposite of this definition? Being unaware or unclear about what's actually happening at this moment, but still judging and shaming ourselves.

Sounds an awful lot like depression to us.

# Try This: STOP Sgt. Mind in His Tracks

STOP is a quick and easy practice to help you get in touch with mindfulness and see things clearly.

- **S**top whatever it is you're doing: put down the book, the iPad, stop moving.

- **T**ake a breath. Really feel the inhale and the exhale.

- **O**bserve what's happening. And when we say "observe," we mean observe what is happening around you and outside of you for a moment, then observe what is really happening inside of you. Are you looking yourself, or is Sgt. Mind showing you?

- **P**roceed with whatever it was you had been doing before.

  You can stop Sgt. Mind anytime you notice him sneaking up on you, or better yet, at regular times of day just to keep him away.

Write down a few times when you might use a practice like STOP with Sgt. Mind—for example, after a disappointment or before going into a stressful situation like a test, performance, game, or party.

_____

_____

_____

_____

# What Mindfulness Is Not

There are many misunderstandings about mindfulness. It doesn't require sitting on funny cushions or going on retreats or even becoming spiritual at all. Cushions or retreats might help some people practice, but you certainly don't need them. For others, mindfulness may feel spiritual, but it doesn't have to be. Mindfulness also doesn't mean becoming passive. You can be very active and be mindful—it's all about being aware of what is happening *now*. And one thing it's definitely not is shutting off your thoughts and feelings by numbing yourself or checking out. It's actually staying very much in contact with them, but in a more flexible, workable way than most people do when they're depressed.

What are some assumptions you made about mindfulness when you first picked up this book? Think back to Sgt. Mind's judgments when he first saw this book. List any reactions here:

_____

_____

_____

_____

_____

Here's a bottom line about mindfulness—are you willing to learn all you can about harnessing the power and opportunity that exists in every moment of your life? Yes, this book is about depression, but more than that, it's about living life to the fullest, getting the most from each moment and experience that comes your way so that you can get the most out of life.

# What Is Positive Psychology?

While mindfulness is about finding and exploring what's in each moment, positive psychology is about making the best of those moments. At its most basic, positive psychology is based on the idea that there is more right than wrong with you. When you're depressed, it often feels like the opposite, and maybe over time you've heard more from other people about what's wrong with you than what's right. By using positive psychology, you can discover and build on the strengths you do have, rather than dwell on the ways depression gets you down.

What evolutionary psychologists (yes, that's a thing—they study why our brains and behavior evolved the way they did) have discovered is that humans are hardwired with a *negativity bias*. This means that we're wired to more often notice the negative and to interpret things in negative ways. This made sense for our ancestors. In a more physically dangerous world, they needed to be scanning constantly for danger. Those who didn't see it didn't survive; those who were extra cautious survived and passed on their genes to the next generation. Psychologist Rick Hanson explains that our minds are like Velcro for anything negative and Teflon for the positives. That negativity bias is also known as Sgt. Mind, giving us twenty-four hours of all-bad news. Instead, we want to change the channel, to actually give us unbiased news, the good and the bad.

If we're depressed, we're even more likely to notice the negative and interpret things in negative ways. When we deliberately practice looking for the positive, we start to rebalance our perspective to fit the world we're living in now. Finding this balance improves our well-being in daily life, and it helps alleviate depression as well by boosting our mood.

Positive psychology is not about pretending everything is great and ignoring the bad, annoying, or dangerous things in life. It's about bringing more attention to the positive, and using specific, concrete strategies to overcome the negativity bias and see things clearly.

If you think about your depression as Sgt. Mind slipping his dark or dirty glasses on your eyes and distorting your vision, mindfulness and positive psychology can help you see more clearly and accurately. Mindfulness cleans the lenses so you can see more clearly, and positive psychology fine-tunes the prescription so you can see farther and more accurately.

Both take some work, especially at first, but over time, with the practices in this book, you can get into good habits about keeping your perspective clear, just like you clean your glasses when they get smudged. We've carefully picked practices that are the most powerful mindfulness and positive-psychology exercises to get the most effect, while still being short and simple. Sometimes small efforts make a big difference. That's what we're going for here, because we know that big efforts can seem extra big when you're depressed.

# A Mindfulness Sampler

In this section, we'll get our feet wet with a few mindfulness and positive-psychology practices. The aim here is to get a sense of these and their effects for you here at the outset. Don't expect them to fix things right off the bat. It will take time and practice. We're just getting a taste of things.

## Try This: Standing Stork

The body is one anchor in the present moment and can be a place to practice concentration and focus. When we are focused on one thing, it's hard for distracting or depressing thoughts—Sgt. Mind's ideas—to get in there and start making us feel worse.

- Stand up straight and find your balance. When you feel stable, lift one leg in the air, and rest the bottom of that foot against the side of your knee, like a stork.

- Try balancing for just a minute. If it's hard, that's fine; it's supposed to be, so just try not to judge yourself. If it's too easy (maybe you're already a great surfer or yoga guru), try balancing on your toes for an extra challenge or, if you're familiar with it, moving into Tree Pose from yoga.

- Experiment a bit with moving your eyes around and then keeping them still and resting on one spot on the floor or wall. Notice what happens to your balance.

- Experiment also with closing your eyes and bringing your mind to strong emotions. Notice what happens to your balance.

- Now sit back down.

While you were focused on balance with your eyes in front of you, were you thinking about anything else? We're guessing you probably weren't!

What happened to your balance when your eyes or mind wandered?

_____

_____

Did you notice any negative self-judgments?

_____

_____

_____

When our minds are focused on one thing in the present, there is little room for depression (or anything else) to sneak in. Of course, if this exercise was hard, you might have heard Sgt. Mind kicking up the self-criticism—that's normal. But as you look back at what you wrote, ask yourself, *Do I have to believe everything he tells me?*

## Try This: 7-11 and 11-7 Breaths

Sometimes when we are depressed it helps if we can lower our energy level a bit and relax. At other times, when we are feeling sluggish, we may want to raise our energy. This simple breathing practice can help in both cases; try it a few times. Ask yourself whether you need to lower or raise your energy.

*Lowering energy:* If you're feeling anxious or overwhelmed, and thoughts are coming too fast, try breathing in for a count of seven, and out for a count of eleven. Repeat for a few breaths. This practice lowers your overall arousal and helps you relax.

*Raising energy:* Often when we are depressed, it can be hard to feel like we have quite enough energy for what we need to do. This breathing practice will raise your energy and awareness somewhat. Try breathing in for a count of eleven and out for a count of seven, and repeat.

**When are some times you can imagine using the 7-11 or 11-7 breath practices?**

_____

_____

_____

# Formal and Informal Practice

A lot of mindfulness teachers talk about training the mind like training the body. Formal physical exercise is going to the gym or sports practice for an hour; informal exercise is walking around and doing things like carrying extra groceries and taking the stairs instead of the elevator.

With mindfulness, you can sit and do formal practice for twenty minutes—maybe a walking or sitting meditation—or do informal practice by bringing your attention to the present moment and back to the task at hand as often as you can remember.

Informal practice can also mean finding moments throughout the day where you can do a simple, short practice that gets you in touch with the present moment, allowing you to step away from judgment, or just focus on the task at hand. No one needs to even know you're practicing in those moments. It can be your healthy little secret.

There are all kinds of moments that can be reminders to come back to your body, your breath, or your mindfulness anchor. Choose one of these moments, and each time it comes up in the next week, try an informal practice like mindful 7-11 breathing or STOPping Sgt. Mind.

- First thing in the morning (before you pick up your phone!)

- As you wait for food to cook or heat up

- While you wait for the bus

- The moment you sit down at your desk, before you start working

- Whenever you have to stop to retie your shoes

- Anytime your phone buzzes or beeps at you

- Whenever you turn on a faucet

- Waiting in line

- Opening a door

- Last thing at night

Basically, anytime you have the impulse to pull out your phone and check your messages or play a game, that's a moment you can check in with yourself.

Mindfulness and positive psychology may not make your depression shrink down and disappear overnight, but they will make you stronger and wiser in relation to it. There's a saying we like that goes "Ask not for a lighter load, but for broader shoulders to carry it." In some ways, mindfulness gives you broader shoulders to carry your load, and positive psychology gives you new perspectives and skills for how to carry it.

# Down and Out or Up and In?

In this chapter, we learned more about mindfulness and positive psychology and how they might help with your depression.

What have you learned from this chapter about how depression gets you *down* in your mood and checking *out* of daily life?

_____

_____

_____

_____

What specific strategies or ideas from this chapter might help you lift your mood *up* and move you *in* toward people and activities?

_____

_____

_____

_____

_____

What one strategy, idea, or tool are you willing to put to use in the next twenty-four hours? Write it here, and commit to doing so.

_____

_____

_____

# chapter 3

# Body-Based Approaches to Depression

There is more wisdom in your body than in your deepest philosophy.

—Friedrich Nietzsche

A healthy body is the foundation for a healthy, happy mind and mood, or at least more manageable ones. Your strong body can help keep Sgt. Mind at bay, but he'll definitely tell you to not bother with some of the physical self-care in this chapter. Chris often jokes with clients that their grandmothers were right—eating, sleeping, and getting exercise are the most important things you can do to take care of yourself. Taking care of your body is important to your physical health as well as your mental health, and your teen years are a good opportunity to get into lifelong habits of physical well-being.

In this chapter, we'll explore the biological approach to managing depression from a number of angles, including sleep, exercise, diet, substance intake, and relaxation. We'll again apply mindfulness and positive psychology to thinking about changes you can make in your life.

# Sleep

We get it—this is a hard one for young people these days. Between finding the time for studying and social life, both of which seem to take more time than in your parents' day, getting a full night's rest is no easy feat. Still, getting the right amount—for most teens, from eight to ten hours—can have a major impact on your mood, not to mention your brain and body's overall functioning for everything you want to do, from athletics to academics to hanging with friends.

Just as important as getting enough sleep is getting regular sleep. For some who are depressed, sleeping too much might actually be part of the problem. This is part of what can be confusing about depression: some folks need to be reminded to go to sleep, some need to be reminded to get up. Getting quality sleep and getting consistent sleep are both important for your mood. So try to find a way to get to sleep and wake up around the same time most days, even if it means not sleeping in quite so much on the weekends. Your body needs the right kind of rest to fight off and keep depression at bay.

How much sleep are you getting on average?

_____

Do you tend to have a similar sleep schedule most of the time?

_____

## Building Good Sleep Habits

Can you adjust anything in your schedule or ask someone to remind you to get a little more sleep? Or, if you're oversleeping, can you set your alarm or have a friend text you to get up? Ask your parent to knock on your door? A number of things can keep your brain and body awake, so keep these points in mind for a good night's sleep "diet":

- Your last significant physical exercise should be at least two hours before bed.

- Have dinner about two to three hours before bed, and stop snacking, or have only very small snacks, after dinner.

- Avoid alcohol, nicotine, caffeine, and other drugs too close to bed.

- Shut off screens an hour before bed; light from LED and TV screens can overstimulate, confuse, and wake up the brain. (We know this is tough, but maybe you can switch to a paper book or magazine.)

- Stop stressful work, studying, planning, and high-drama socializing within an hour of bed.

- Have a relaxing ritual before sleep; for example, writing in a journal, reading something inspirational, or doing some relaxing breath or body techniques like the ones described throughout this book.

- Sleep in a bedroom that is dark, cool, and quiet (consider a white noise machine).

- Aim to get to sleep and wake up around the same time each day.

You may find yourself looking at this list and saying something Sgt. Mind-y to yourself like, *Yeah, yeah—I know I should do this stuff, but it won't help and I'll never keep up with it anyway.* Know that such thinking is completely normal. Very few people (even the two of us) do all these things every night.

You have all sorts of habits in your daily routine that you've built up over time. With a bit of deliberate effort, you can certainly make some changes to your nightly routine to get some good sleep habits going as well.

# Meditation Before Sleep

Distracting and depressing thoughts can be quite overwhelming, and often when we slow down, it seems like they speed up. It's reasonable to be concerned that if we make some mental space, we might also be making room for Sgt. Mind to show up and start chattering at us. The temptation can then be to distract ourselves before sleep, to keep negative thoughts at bay. But of course the thoughts are only part of the problem. The bigger challenge is that we tend to believe our thoughts, when perhaps we'd be better off letting them go, rather than staying with them.

## Try This: Floating Leaves on a Stream

Lie down, and allow yourself to get comfortable.

Imagine yourself sitting overlooking a beautiful river or stream, perhaps one flowing through a flowery meadow, the mountains, or maybe a deep, ancient forest. Take a breath, and allow everything to become more vivid: the colors, the sounds, even the smells of nature. As you sit and watch the stream flow by, you notice things floating along in the stream or on its surface. Leaves drift past, then disappear around the next bend.

You may start to notice that even in this beautiful place, thoughts, worries, and uncomfortable sensations are still present from time to time. Each time you become aware of one, imagine shrinking the thought down and placing it on a leaf floating past, and then watching it drift away. Some thoughts may get stuck, circling in an eddy or tangled up, but eventually they will float away. The key is to keep shrinking down the thoughts and letting them drift away. From time to time you may find yourself floating alongside the thoughts, getting farther downstream, but all you need to do is just notice where you've drifted and pull yourself back to shore, over and over. Just place your thoughts on the leaves and let them go, as many times as you need to.

Was there any pattern to where your mind went, or did it seem random?

_____

_____

If you don't find leaves on a river helpful, there are other images that might work; for example, watching traffic going past on a highway or bridge from a distant height, or noticing clouds floating past in the sky, or watching fish swim by in an aquarium.

# Exercise

The research is clear—for many forms of depression, getting exercise is at least as helpful as medication. Other evidence shows that exercise not only boosts your mood but also gives you more energy and helps you focus and think more clearly and creatively, sleep better, and regulate your appetite. It doesn't even take much; researchers now say that from ten to thirty minutes of moderately intense exercise a few times a week is often as good as more intense working out, at least for your mood.

Of course, mustering the energy to do anything (let alone exercising) is tough when depression is weighing you down. And we don't want to make exercise another chore for you to stress about. But exercise doesn't have to mean running around the track or joining a varsity sports team. There are plenty of ways to exercise that are just as beneficial to your mind and body as competitive sports. It just means moving your body. Even standing up while you read or do work can help.

Some forms of exercise have the added benefit of getting you outside, into the world of fresh air, sunlight, and color. There is increasing evidence that just being in nature can lift your mood and boost your psychological well-being, resilience, and even interpersonal skills. And getting some sunlight (within reason) is especially important if your depression tends to be worse in the winter, as it is for people with seasonal affective disorder.

You can likely find something that allows your body to move and your mind to let go of worries. Is there anything on this list more appealing than traditional sports? Use the blank lines to add your own ideas.

| | |
|---|---|
| Biking | Skating |
| Boating | Skiing |
| Dancing | Snowboarding |
| Fencing | Surfing |
| Fitness-oriented video games | Swimming |
| Gymnastics | Walking |
| Hiking | Weight lifting |
| Martial arts | Yardwork or housework |
| Parkour | Yoga |
| Playing catch | _____ |
| Rock climbing | _____ |

Which of the activities on this list can you do in the next week?

_____

_____

_____

# Getting Motivated to Move

Getting (and staying) motivated for even the most fun, rewarding, or effective exercise is hardly easy. For that reason, what we suggest is to start small, especially if it's been a while since you've exercised. Just walking for twenty minutes a day can boost your mood significantly. One young man Chris works with listens to stand-up comedy while he does his walk. Is there an interesting podcast, audiobook, or music you can listen to? If you make an exercise playlist of just five or six songs, you can easily get twenty or thirty minutes of even a mild workout. And one great way to get yourself to exercise is to do it with someone else. Meet a friend for a jog, or ask if friends, teachers, therapists, and other people want to take a walk instead of sitting around when you spend time with them.

List a few people you might be willing and able to exercise with, or even take a walk with, in the coming week:

_____

_____

_____

Technology won't make you exercise, but it can make exercise more appealing. Consider getting a fitness tracker device or app for your phone. Plenty of yoga, tai chi, Pilates, and other workout videos can be borrowed from the library, but just as many are online for free. There are also workout video games, including sports like tennis or bowling, or activities like dancing and aerobics.

Are there any exercise apps, videos, or video games that you've enjoyed in the past, or think you might enjoy? List them here:

_____

_____

_____

_____

# Making Time to Exercise

Think about your schedule. Are there times you can fit in some formal exercise? A yoga or dance class, an intramural sport, a trip to the gym? Can you get someone to go with you? Pick an activity, and perhaps a person, and then put it into your calendar or phone. It may seem silly to schedule in your exercise, but for many people (including these two authors), if it's not in the calendar, it will never get done!

Do you have appointments where you usually take the elevator when you could take the stairs? Are there times you can walk when you usually catch a ride? Write those down here, and put a reminder in your phone or calendar for the next opportunity you might have for "informal" exercise.

_____

_____

_____

# Walking

You may feel completely inactive, but chances are you're at least walking some places, and that's some exercise in itself. There may also be some ways to do more walking—to school, work, friends' houses, or your appointments and activities.

While it won't give you a high-calorie cardio burn, mindful walking will get you moving and reinforce your awareness of your body—both crucial to helping you shake depression loose. There are all kinds of ways to do mindful walking, but for this book we'll share just a few with you.

# Try This: Mindful Walking

Mindful walking really just means being present and noticing all the sensations and aspects of walking. Once you get the hang of it, you can bring mindfulness to walking not just in your house but also in the world around you.

- Find a space in your house, dorm, or yard about ten feet long to walk back and forth, or a circle about that wide. You can walk in lines or in circles; it's up to you.

- Stand up straight with your feet about hips' width apart, and feel some uplift and strength in your chest and torso. Take a deep breath in, and let it out as you relax your shoulders.

- Slowly lift your right foot and place it in front of you. As you do so, try to remain aware of all the sensations in your body. Notice all the tiny movements of the muscles as you balance, and feel your weight shifting as your left heel peels off the ground and you move that foot. Just take a few steps like this, noticing all the sensations.

- As in any mindfulness practice, just notice where your thoughts go and gently bring your awareness back to your movement, the anchor for this practice.

- Set a time, and try walking like this for five or ten minutes.

A positive-psychology variation on mindful walking is to bring deliberate attention to your surroundings, intentionally noticing what's beautiful, interesting, or pleasing in the environment where you're walking. This practice starts to shift our perception of the world, cleaning Sgt. Mind's lenses of negative perception so that our minds break the habit of looking for the bad rather than the good in the world.

# Brief Mindful Yoga

When our bodies are flexible and strong, our minds become more flexible and strong, happier, and less depressed and likely to fall for Sgt. Mind's best lines. Yoga can be great for physical and mental flexibility, and it doesn't have to mean putting on a special outfit or leaving the house. Just some comfortable loose clothes, even pajamas, are fine for these poses. You don't even need a mat. If your floor is soft, great; if it's hard, lay down a towel or two, or maybe a small rug.

Don't push yourself too hard, and check with your doctor to make sure these poses are okay for your body. You can do these three poses in order, or you can just pick the ones that feel best to you. If you want some help visualizing these movements, there are about a million videos online you can watch.

## COBRA

This opening, empowering pose can quickly change the way you feel and bring up your energy level.

- Start by lying facedown. Keep your palms flat, fingers forward, beneath your shoulders.

- Widen your fingers, and press your palms down so that your torso lifts off the ground. Rotate your shoulders back and down so they don't bunch up next to your ears.

- Continue pushing on your palms, letting your whole torso rise until your arms are as straight as possible. Keep your feet, legs, and hips on the ground or mat beneath you. Lift and open your chest as your chin points upward and outward.

- Hold this posture for three or four breaths. As you hold it, notice how your body feels, and also pay attention to your mind and emotional state.

- Gently lower yourself back down.

If that feels like enough, just rest there. If you want to keep going, you can sequence in the next pose, or do it separately.

## DOWNWARD-FACING DOG

This pose can feel really centering and powerful as you stretch your body out, balance yourself, and hold yourself up.

- Start on your hands and knees, hands directly under your shoulders and knees beneath your hips.

- Curl your toes under, shifting weight back, and press up against your hands, lifting your hips toward the ceiling. Your body should be an upside-down V shape.

- See if you can hold this position for three or more breaths. Again, notice how you feel in both your body and mind, as you push downward and lift your body with your own power and strength.

- Lower your knees to the floor, followed by the rest of your upper body.

Again, if you feel good with that pose, just rest. If you want to keep going, move on to Upward-Facing Dog.

## UPWARD-FACING DOG

Like Cobra, this posture opens the chest and stretches out the back.

- Start facing downward with hands at your sides, allowing your body to stretch out and relax.

- Rest your palms on the floor next to your chest, and shift your gaze outward, directly in front of you.

- As you inhale, squeeze your shoulder blades together and then exhale as you press upward on your hands, raising your torso.

- Pull your shoulder blades back and lift your rib cage upward and outward.

- Hold again for a few breaths. Notice how you feel. Slowly lower yourself, and rest lying down.

How did these postures feel physically and emotionally? Which felt most empowering?

_____

_____

_____

If you had a favorite, which was it?

_____

Which ones can you make time for in the next week?

_____

_____

# Eating

Like sleep, our appetite usually goes in two directions when we are depressed: overeating for comfort, or undereating because we don't have any appetite and nothing appeals to us. Healthy food is the best fuel for keeping depression in check and keeping your body and mind fit for remaining stronger and smarter than Sgt. Mind.

## *Overeating*

Food can be very comforting, but often the more comforting the food, the less healthy it is. That's not to say that you have to be perfect about eating, but a few changes in diet can help your mood. It's important to learn to distinguish between eating for sustenance and health (to feel better in the long run) and eating for emotional reasons (to feel better in the moment). The following chart can help you understand the differences.

| Emotional Eating | Healthy Eating |
| --- | --- |
| Eating just when you're emotional; for example, sad, stressed, frustrated, or bored | Eating when your body is telling you it's hungry; for example, your stomach is growling or your energy is low |
| Eating at random times | Eating at regular times |
| Eating past full and ignoring, or not recognizing, your body's signals | Stopping when your body tells you it's done |
| Eating foods that are emotionally comforting | Eating foods that are nutritionally healthy |
| Eating only certain foods, bingeing | Eating a variety of foods in a balanced way, in moderation |
| Wandering around looking for food | Planning your next meal or snack in advance |
| Experiencing sudden cravings | Experiencing slow-building hunger |
| Finding only a few foods satisfying | Finding many foods satisfying |
| Often feeling guilty afterward | Usually feeling good afterward |
| Eating in secret | Feeling comfortable and unashamed eating around others |

As you review this chart, do you notice any of the healthy or emotional eating habits jumping out at you? We've all occasionally drowned our sorrows in a pint of ice cream or bag of chips, or have otherwise resorted to some emotional eating. That does not mean you have an eating disorder. It's just that for some people, relying too heavily on food for coping with difficult emotions may be a sign of a more worrisome pattern.

Many teens, especially those with depression, have a complicated relationship to food and body image. Our culture sends mixed messages to everyone, and so you're not alone if you're confused about food and health. And some people feel guilty about eating even healthy foods or feel awkward eating in front of others no matter what they're eating. These might or might not be signs of an eating disorder. It can be helpful to talk and reflect about what food and your body mean to you with trusted friends, family, or professionals.

Here are other suggestions related to nutrition:

- Balanced meals with lots of veggies and not too many sweets provide the most nutrients possible to help your brain and body function at their best.

- Try foods that are high in protein and fiber and lower in carbs, which can contribute to ups and downs in mood.

- You also might check with a nutritionist or your doctor to be sure you're getting enough nutrients; you might need vitamin supplements. Some deficiencies, like vitamins B and D, iron, and others, can affect your mood.

- If you follow a certain diet, or are vegetarian or vegan, it can be hard to maintain a balanced diet if the others in your family eat differently. Again, your doctor or nutritionist can help you eat a balanced diet that will help your depression.

What are your "emotional eating" triggers, if this is a problem for you?

_____

_____

_____

_____

# Not Having an Appetite

For many teens with depression, overeating is not a problem, because they hardly have any appetite. You might fall into this category. Eating when you're not hungry is a true challenge. Many young people skip breakfast or lunch, and yes, we're going to sound like your parents when we tell you it's important to eat three healthy meals a day!

If you can't work up an appetite, try some foods that are easy to digest: trail mix, bananas, yogurt, toast, or dried fruit. These are pretty gentle on your system and give you the energy you need to think clearly. They also give you the energy needed to exercise and talk, and give your body the signals it needs to sleep properly—all of which can help you fight off the dark clouds of depression.

One young woman Chris worked with could not boost her appetite. She finally found it helpful to resign herself to the idea that eating food was like taking medicine: "I don't like taking my pills, I don't like eating my breakfast, and I don't like getting exercise and talking to people, but they're all medicine for my depression." Maybe you've never been a breakfast eater; you don't have to commit to eating breakfast forever, but try it for a few weeks the same way you would try medication.

Exercise can also help. Try scheduling exercise before mealtime to work up an appetite.

Right now, are you eating three balanced meals a day? What did you eat within the last twenty-four hours? And how does it stack up against the recommendations in this chapter? (Be honest with yourself!)

_____

_____

_____

_____

If there is nothing that seems appealing, what are some foods that are at least tolerable, even when you have no appetite or a nervous stomach?

_____

_____

_____

_____

What are some of your favorite healthy foods that you can eat in the next week? Can you get some healthy snacks, or ask your parents to pick some up for you?

_____

_____

_____

_____

## Eating Mindfully

Ideally we'd make our meals the anchor of awareness and bring mindfulness to all aspects of eating. It's nearly impossible to do this with every meal, but try to set aside some time every week to either have a meal or snack in a mindful way. For your other meals, you could just eat the first few bites mindfully.

# Try This: Mindful Eating

Before you even take a bite, bring mindful awareness to preparing the meal. Notice details of how the food looks, the colors and textures, as you place it on the plate in an appealing way. Notice the sounds of preparation—the opening of cabinets and clinking of plates—and the smells of the food itself. Remain aware of the physical and emotional sensations in your mind and body, signals of hunger, and emotions that come along with preparing your food.

- Sit down at a table, and eat from a plate, putting away phones, screens, and other distractions. As you sit down, take a deep breath and just look again at your plate. As you eat, just eat, at a pace slow enough to maintain awareness of the physical, sensory, and emotional aspects of the process.

- To slow down, it can help to set your utensils down between bites, lean back between bites, and sip your water or beverage. Notice after each swallow how your body feels.

- When you're done, lean back and spend a few moments just noticing sensations in your body. Are you full? Satisfied? More than full?

As you practice eating mindfully from time to time, you'll better recognize your body's signals for when it is hungry, what kind of food it really needs, and how much. You'll eat because your body needs it, not because your depression wants an escape. Over time, your body and mind will become better able to maintain your mood when they get the nutrition they need.

Try eating a meal or part of a meal mindfully as described here. What did you notice about the experience?

_____

_____

_____

_____

# Substance Intake

So this is the part where we talk about cutting down on nonprescribed chemicals—alcohol, drugs, nicotine, and caffeine. Like everything else in this book, we aren't judging the choices you make or suggesting you follow our advice forever. We just recommend that you make some changes to see for yourself if that affects your depression. And if you prefer not to write down your answers to the questions at the end of this section, you can think about them instead.

The fact is, drugs and alcohol might work in the short term to help you feel better, but the medium- and long-term effects on your body and mind only weaken your ability to keep Sgt. Mind quiet and depression away. If you're hungover or otherwise recovering from substances, all your energy is going into that, leaving none to help you also recover from depression. Caffeine and nicotine might boost your energy when you're feeling sluggish, but it can be easy to get dependent on them without realizing it. They also can raise your stress and anxiety level, which hardly helps anything.

Another risk arises if you're also taking medication. Most antidepressants don't work effectively when combined with drugs and alcohol, and many can have dangerous interactions. If you're taking medication, check in with your prescriber about interactions.

What's your substance intake like these days? Is it more than you'd like it to be, or more than your friends, family, or health care providers think is healthy for someone with depression?

_____

_____

_____

_____

What are the benefits of using these substances (for example, socializing with others, temporarily shutting off bad feelings)?

_____

_____

_____

_____

What might your use of these substances be costing you (for example, less money, more conflict with your family)?

_____

_____

_____

_____

Is there room to cut down? Are you willing to take a break altogether for a few weeks to see if it makes a difference in your overall mood?

_____

_____

If you take medication, like some people with depression, are you taking it as prescribed, regularly, and daily? If you forget often, what is one way you can remember (for example, by leaving a note on the bathroom mirror or setting an alarm)?

_____

_____

_____

# Relaxation

One of the most important ways to recover from any illness, including depression, is to relax. Stress basically makes everything worse, and that means both your physical health and your mental health. If you're fighting both stress and depression, you're starting with a major disadvantage. Finding some ways to reduce stress and relax more will free up energy to help you manage your depression. Of course, this is easier said than done. A 2014 study found that teenagers are more stressed out than any other age group in the United States, so you're not alone.

Here's some good news: Mindfulness and positive-psychology practices are some of the best and fastest ways to reduce stress. Healthy relaxation allows the body to recover and recharge with the energy it needs to fight depression.

What are some ways you like to relax? We all have different ones, so use the blank lines to add your own ideas.

Being creative (writing, painting, drawing)

Calling a supportive friend

Dancing

Doing a crossword or sudoku

Going for a walk

Listening to music or comedy

Massaging yourself (or getting someone to give you a massage)

Meditating

People watching

Playing with a stress toy

Shopping

Taking a bath or shower

Taking care of your plants or pets

Telling jokes

Trying aromatherapy (smelling some spices, coffee, tea, flowers, lotions, or oils)

_____

_____

Which of these can you fit into your schedule?

_____

_____

_____

_____

_____

# *Muscle Relaxation*

**When we need more than just a relaxing activity, a formal relaxation practice can help.**

## Try This: Mindful Muscle Relaxation

You can read along as you do this exercise, but you also might like taking turns with a friend, guiding each other. You can also record yourself (or someone else) reading the scripts aloud and then listen later.

- Find a comfortable place to sit or lie down where you won't be disturbed for about fifteen minutes. Put on some comfy clothes, dim the lights, and if you like, put on some soothing music. Allow your body to sink into the surface beneath you.

- Start by taking three deep breaths. With each in-breath, imagine breathing in relaxing energy, and with each out-breath, imagine breathing out any tension and stress. Bring your awareness to your body. If your attention wanders, just notice where it has gone, and then gently bring it back.

- On the next breath, point your toes outward until you feel a stretch. Hold this for a few breaths, noticing the sensations, and then let go. As you release, notice what it feels like to let go of tension.

- Now curl your feet upward toward you, again feeling the stretch and the tension in your ankles and up the front of your calves. Hold for a few breaths once more and then release, aware of the changing sensations.

- Over the next few minutes, gradually work your way up through the main muscle groups of your body, simply tensing and holding, and then releasing and noticing what each feels like, both physically and emotionally.

- Tense and release the muscles in each area of your lower body—your calves, then thighs, then hips and buttocks.

- Bring special attention to your lower back, stomach area, and upper back, as these are places we carry stress.

- Your hands and fingers can be stretched out and balled up before moving up to your biceps and triceps.

- If your mind wanders, just notice that and breathe in relaxation, breathe out any tension, and bring your focus back into the body.

- Your neck and shoulders also hold stress, so notice the sensations and emotions of tension as you tighten and then release them.

- Moving up to your face muscles, just be aware of how your face feels from the inside, then scrunch your forehead down, eyes squeezing shut, and make your face into a scowl. Notice this experience for a breath or two, and then the experience of relaxing your face.

- Lastly, tense your jaw muscles tight. Really feel the tension here in mind and body for a few breaths, and then just…let…go…and feel the release and relaxation.

Take a moment now and scan through your whole body, noticing how it feels at the end of this exercise. As you return to your day, you can return to some of this relaxation just by tensing and releasing a few muscles that are storing any tension.

# *Short Check-Ins and Relaxations*

Of course, you don't always have twenty minutes to do a long mindful relaxation practice. There are a few short relaxation practices that might help, and their acronyms—CALM and HALT—make them easy to remember.

## Try This: HALT! and Check Your Needs

When we lose track of our most basic needs, we often lose track of our moods as well. But we can check in with ourselves from time to time and see what our needs are, or what may be affecting our moods. Every so often, try to mindfully halt what you're doing and ask yourself if you're feeling any of the following:

- **H**ungry—Are you feeling hungry? Does your body need to eat?

- **A**ngry or Anxious—Are you feeling either angry or anxious? Is there a way you can soothe these strong, agitated feelings?

- **L**onely—Are you feeling alone? Can you reach out to anyone to feel less lonely right now, even with just a text?

- **T**ired—Are you feeling sleepy or sluggish? Is there a way you can respond mindfully to this feeling?

## Try This: CALM—A Short Mindful Body Check-In

You might find that not taking care of your body's needs leads to your mood dropping and your depression worsening. A few times a day, it can be helpful to check in with some parts of your body. This practice can give you early warnings about your mood.

- **C**hest—Notice any tension in your chest, and the speed of your heart and breath. What are they telling you about your emotional and physical state at this moment?

- **A**rms—Tightness in your arms and fists might reveal some frustration and tension. Can you give these muscles a quick squeeze and then let go?

- **L**egs—When your legs are restless, perhaps vibrating like a jackhammer, it's another sign that you may need to relax and let go of stress. Again, you can give the muscles a squeeze, and then just let go.

- **M**ind—What's going on with your mind? Are you noticing stressful thoughts? Can you take a few mindful breaths, or connect with the present moment in some other way to de-stress yourself?

**What are some times you can use these short check-ins?**

_____

_____

_____

_____

# Down and Out or Up and In?

By now, you've hopefully learned some basic skills for mindfully taking care of your body in order to take care of your depression. We covered some of the basics of physical self-care, bringing mindfulness into sleep, eating, physical exercise, and de-stressing your body with relaxation.

What have you learned from this chapter about how depression gets you *down* in your mood so that you're checking *out* of daily life?

_____

_____

_____

_____

What specific strategies or ideas from this chapter might help you lift your mood *up* and move you *in* toward people and activities?

_____

_____

_____

_____

What one strategy, idea, or tool are you willing to put to use in the next twenty-four hours? Write it here, and commit to doing so.

_____

_____

_____

# chapter 4

# Psychological Approaches to Depression

Your thoughts can be your most powerful servant, or most terrible master.

—Japanese proverb

Sgt. Mind, the "voice" of depression, likes to talk to you in ways that make things worse. Even though he's trying to protect you from bad stuff, he ends up getting in the way of your doing things you'd really like to do (or at least used to like). These depressed thoughts from Sgt. Mind can spark some really tough feelings as well, feelings so big and dark it can seem impossible to get past them.

In this chapter, we learn more about what's happening inside (your thoughts and emotions) with these experiences we call depression, and we'll explore the ways to mindfully work with your internal landscape using mindfulness and positive-psychology strategies.

## Mood Tracking

Tracking your mood will give you the information you need to better manage your daily thoughts, feelings, and behavior. The weird part is, studies show that when people keep track of how they feel, the mere fact that they're observing and paying attention to themselves tends to help things start to improve.

All emotions vary in their strength, from strong to weak. When your mood is low, it can sometimes be hard to notice small changes in your feelings. That's a main reason to develop the skill of mood tracking—it will help you notice when your feelings are changing (which happens more often than you might think) and help you learn what to do to change your mood for the better. Let's start with getting some information about your experiences with emotions.

Think of some past experiences where you felt bad, upset, or distressed, or were experiencing a negative mood in some way. Look for one experience that was the most significant in terms of how bad you felt, and then other situations that were less intense. List five of these:

1. _____

2. _____

3. _____

4. _____

5. _____

Now, recall five experiences from the past where you were feeling good. Include the time where you felt the best you can remember, as well as other positive experiences—perhaps successes, graduations, parties, vacations, or other memories (but not ones that might feel complicated now, like an amazing conversation with an ex).

1. _____

2. _____

3. _____

4. _____

5. _____

If you're stuck, ask for help from someone you trust.

Once you have your lists, put these ten items in order from "feeling very good" to "feeling very bad" and write them on this Feelings Thermometer. Here's an important point: The thermometer is about feelings, not facts, so don't worry about getting it just right. It's a helpful reminder of the point that feelings aren't facts!

## My Feelings Thermometer

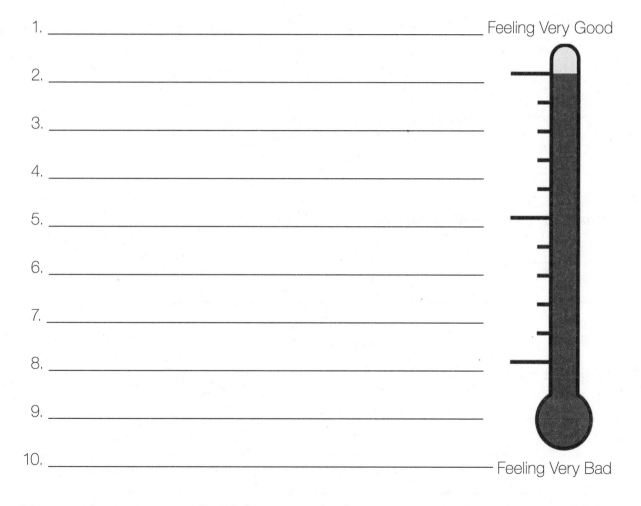

1. _____ Feeling Very Good

2. _____

3. _____

4. _____

5. _____

6. _____

7. _____

8. _____

9. _____

10. _____ Feeling Very Bad

You now have a personalized thermometer that you can use to track your mood, and you can download additional copies of the form at http://www.newharbin ger.com/33827 (see the back of this book for instructions). You can compare a current situation to your thermometer, and give it a number rating. For example, if the current situation feels similar to the past situation you ranked 5, you'll give it a 5 rating, and so on.

## Try This: Mindfulness of Mood

Find an upright, comfortable posture. Close your eyes and focus on your breathing for three or four breaths. Bring to mind the experience you rated as 1 on your thermometer. Spend a few moments noticing the sensations in your body, paying attention to anything that pops up in your awareness—tingling, discomfort, itching, whatever. Just notice exactly where you feel it and what it feels like.

Now bring to mind the experience you rated as 10. Spend a few moments again noticing where you feel any sensations in your body.

Don't worry about doing anything in particular. The exercise is to just notice the sensations in your body when you bring up the memory of a past experience, whether positive or negative.

What did "feeling bad" actually feel like in your mind and body?

_____

_____

_____

What did "feeling good" actually feel like?

_____

_____

_____

Use the table below to list situations, what you were thinking and how you felt, and your actions for each day of the week. It might look like a lot of work, but once you get in the habit, it really takes only a minute or two to fill it out.

# The Daily Mood Tracker

| | Situation | Thought | Bodily Sensation | Emotion | Rating (0–10) | Action |
|---|---|---|---|---|---|---|
| Example | Criticized during lunch by my friend Sam | "I'm such a loser and this just proves it." | Tight jaw and neck and heavy feeling in stomach | Sad | 4 | Ignore a text from Sam |
| Monday | | | | | | |
| Tuesday | | | | | | |
| Wednesday | | | | | | |

| | Situation | Thought | Bodily Sensation | Emotion | Rating (0–10) | Action |
|---|---|---|---|---|---|---|
| Thursday | | | | | | |
| Friday | | | | | | |
| Saturday | | | | | | |
| Sunday | | | | | | |

Try using the form for a week, and see what patterns emerge. If it feels helpful, download additional copies at http://www.newharbinger.com/33827, continue tracking your mood, and share it with someone.

Here's an important reason for doing mood tracking: it gives you hard evidence that helps debunk whatever harsh, judging, and unhelpful stuff Sgt. Mind is spewing at you. Sgt. Mind will say that you, others, or the world are "bad," "ridiculous," or "hopeless" in some way and that everything that's negative is absolutely horrible. Mood tracking helps you slow down, see things more clearly, and not be so extreme (and negative) in your thinking. Slowing down and getting more fact based in your thinking has the effect of helping your feelings slow down (and be less intensely negative) as well. It helps your mood shift for the better.

In the next section, we look even more directly at the role thoughts play, and how you can manage them more effectively.

# Working with Thoughts

Taking a long, hard, curious look at how your thoughts affect you can help you get a handle on how depression grips you. In this section, we'll help you understand some principles about thoughts and then give you a menu of strategies for working with the tough ones.

In this oft-repeated parable, a powerful samurai warrior comes to the Master in search of the secret of life.

"Tell me the nature of heaven and hell," demanded the samurai.

The Master sat calmly and slowly looked up at the samurai, whose armor was gleaming in the morning light. The Master smiled. "And why should I tell a despicable, worthless ant of a man such as yourself?" he said. "What makes you—a lowly worm—think you deserve to know of such things?"

With a swift swirl of rage, the warrior drew his sword and held it above the Master's head, poised to strike down this thin, grizzled man who had dared insult him.

Just before the samurai could bring down death on him, the Master pointed up to him and said, "That's hell."

The samurai dropped his sword and wrung his shaking hands. He could not believe that in a flash of anger he had almost been willing to murder a defenseless holy man. Tears dripped onto his intricately carved armor. He was fully aware of this man sitting before him whose words had, in a mere moment, taught him about the extremes of his impulses.

"That's heaven," said the Master.

Thoughts, particularly the rigid rants of Sgt. Mind, shape our reactions to daily life. A lavish cruise or the line for lunch in the cafeteria can equally be hell or heaven depending on your thoughts, your companions, and other factors.

## Taking an Inventory of Your Difficult Thoughts

Sgt. Mind has one perspective on the world, others, yourself, and your prospects for the future. He's critical and quick to judge, and he gives you plenty of reasons for why things feel bad and whose fault that is. Here's the thing—we're going to learn to put some new lenses in Sgt. Mind's glasses.

In the space below, write about a time when you're fairly certain your thoughts played a big role in how bad the experience felt to you:

_____

_____

_____

_____

_____

How do your thoughts play a role in how you end up feeling? If you're thinking dark or rigid thoughts, how do you end up feeling?

_____

_____

_____

_____

_____

_____

## Try This: Chocolate Cake Meditation

Look at a clock or stopwatch, and for just thirty seconds try your best to not (not even once) think about rich, thick, fudgy, delicious chocolate cake. Ready... set...go!

Now take a moment and close your eyes. Notice the feeling of your breathing. Don't think about breathing, but gently feel it. Do this for just a few breaths and then look at your clock again. For the next thirty seconds, continue to notice the feeling of your breathing. If you happen to notice thoughts about rich, thick, fudgy, delicious chocolate cake, that's absolutely fine. Just notice them and gently bring yourself back to the feeling of your breathing. Ready... set...go!

What did you notice? Which way of managing your thoughts about chocolate cake felt easier? Which took more effort? Most people find it tiring to try to force themselves not to think about something. They find it much better to gently notice their thoughts and not struggle with them. Mindfulness helps with that— it helps you learn not to believe everything you think. It's learning to mindfully notice and watch your thoughts instead of fighting them. When we practice (with the techniques below), Sgt. Mind loses some of his power.

Without thinking too much about it, and being as honest and thoughtful as possible, how would you finish the following sentences?

As a friend I have to…

_____

As a family member I must always…

_____

As a good student I need to…

_____

Imagine we have a crystal ball that can tell your future. Imagine that you've shared the sentences you just completed—your "rules" for how you're supposed to be in the important roles in your life. We've given the crystal ball a careful glance and seen that you're going to repeatedly break these "rules," doing pretty much the opposite of what you've said you must always do.

What shows up in your thoughts now? What would Sgt. Mind say about you if you break your own rules? Write down these thoughts here:

_____

_____

_____

_____

This is your initial inventory of "difficult" thoughts. They probably have a lot to do with your depression.

# A Menu of Strategies

So now let's review a menu of techniques for mixing things up with Sgt. Mind. This is a menu like one at a restaurant. You don't order everything on it every time you visit; you try different things until you realize what your favorites are, what works for you.

With this menu, the goal is to explore and even play with your thoughts—the more playful, the better. Being playful with these thoughts does *not* mean that things aren't serious, or that things haven't been painful or troubling for you. Playfulness here is not meant to make light of, or laugh off, your very real experience. Instead, it's a deliberate, powerful choice on your part, a choice to observe your own experience and perhaps learn from it, more clearly and realistically than looking though Sgt. Mind's lenses.

## DRAWING DEPRESSION

If you're willing, imagine Depression is sitting with you in an empty chair nearby. Try to imagine Depression as vividly as possible.

What is he or she (or it) wearing? Imagine gestures and tone of voice. How big or small? Is there movement? Use the space provided to draw or write.

Now review your list of difficult thoughts. Feel the words as much as possible. How do you see them in your imagination? Hear them? Touch them? When you put the thoughts and words on the chair and notice what they look like, does it change how they feel to you? Do you have more or less ability to choose what you want to do next?

## LET IT GO

All thoughts and feelings will eventually change and pass. Hard to remember, but it's true. Try this visualization meditation with your thoughts.

Sit upright, with your hands resting comfortably on your lap. Gently allow your eyes to close. For the next five minutes, simply watch your thoughts as they pass through your awareness. There are a number of images you can use for thoughts lingering and eventually passing; pick one that works for you:

- A cloud passing by in the sky

- Leaves blowing across your path

- Raindrops being cleared away by windshield wipers

- Specks of dust drifting in a ray of sun, then floating away

- Twigs floating downstream in a river

- Cars driving past on the highway

What happened to your difficult thoughts over the course of the five minutes? Did things change or stay exactly the same? Does it help or hurt for you to grip these thoughts in your mind?

## SAY, SAY, SAY

What is the most startling, dramatic, intense word or phrase that Sgt. Mind uses when you're getting tripped up in thinking about your life? Sit for a few moments in silence and allow that word or phrase to emerge in your mind. Perhaps it's a word that someone used in reference to you at school? Maybe a not-so-nice label that you've slapped on yourself? Whatever it is, write it here:

_____

_____

_____

As silly as it sounds, take this word (or phrase) and repeat it aloud over and over as fast as you can for at least thirty seconds. What happens to the word after you've done this? What happens to its meaning after you've repeated it in this way? What has shifted in your experience of its sting? Is there any new distance between the word and your feelings?

_____

_____

_____

## TUNING OUT TEACHER

Imagine that your dark thoughts are coming from a particularly difficult teacher during a lecture in class at school. Watch that teacher up at the front of the classroom shouting your thoughts at everyone. Sgt. Mind is that teacher—convincing, isn't he?

Now, imagine turning away from Sgt. Mind and looking around the room. Notice chairs, windows, the floor, the ceiling; notice your own body, your breathing—in short, notice everything else along with your thoughts. Imagine the lights brightening in the room and then imagine them dimming until they go out altogether while Sgt. Mind is going on and on. What happens? How does your experience shift?

_____

_____

_____

_____

_____

## THOUGHT BREATHING

Sitting in a calm, relaxed position with your eyes closed, bring to mind some challenging thoughts, and watch as they pass in front of your awareness. As they appear, breathe slowly and deeply into the thoughts. Try breathing space all around these thoughts, as if you're creating more sky around the clouds. Keep creating space in and around your thoughts in this way for a minute or two.

When you're ready, slowly open your eyes. Is there more or less space around these thoughts now than before you closed your eyes?

# Positivity Skills

If you know anything about gardening, you know that growing big, beautiful flowers requires compost to provide the plants with nutrients they need for flowers to bloom. What is compost? It's basically garbage—rotten fruit, lawn trimmings, and the like—that enriches the soil. More garbage means better flowers. The same is true of bad situations that are part of life. If you're willing to step back and take a long, thoughtful look at things, you'll see there might be some "compost" in your bad situation that could grow into something worthwhile.

Activist Malala Yousafzai took a devastating murder attempt against her as a chance to spread the word about education for women and girls, and won a Nobel Peace Prize in the process. Basketball great Michael Jordan got cut from his high school team and decided to just practice harder. Swimmer Michael Phelps decided his ADHD diagnosis was a good reason to start exercising and became the most medaled athlete in Olympic history.

You don't have to win an international award or be a celebrity or superstar athlete to transform a would-be setback into something positive. As therapists, we've seen many everyday people transform pain into something positive. Tom took his breakup as an opportunity to deepen his other friendships. Jessica took being grounded for a weekend as a chance for songwriting and practicing the guitar without distractions. Eliza's brother was diagnosed with Asperger's disorder, and she took the opportunity to educate others in her community about the diagnosis and raise money for the cause.

Bring to mind a negative event, conversation, or recent episode; nothing too big to start with, just something small or medium. Consider your difficult situation and ask yourself:

- Even though this is upsetting and hard, what could I learn from it if I looked back in a week? In a year? In ten years?

- Even though this is not what I want, how might I (or maybe others) benefit if I stop fighting with it so hard?

Write a note to Sgt. Mind thanking him for a recent difficult situation you experienced. Despite what he says, how might this situation be of positive importance in some way?

_____

_____

_____

_____

_____

_____

_____

## Recognizing Your Strengths

There is much more to you than just your depression. Positive psychology starts with the idea that our strengths are more important to recognize than our so-called weaknesses. Our strengths are also what we can rely on, and probably already have relied on, to get us through difficult times. Instead of starting with what we don't like about ourselves, we can start with what we do like.

What strengths have you relied on in the past?

_____

_____

_____

_____

For many of us, looking in the mirror is not a fun experience—we feel not good enough and wish things were more ideal, particularly if we're looking at ourselves through Sgt. Mind's dark glasses. We have to learn to question what Sgt. Mind tells us about our physical, emotional, and social reflection. If you're already feeling depressed, it doesn't make sense to focus on the things you feel are weaknesses, or not good enough.

Let's start instead with strengths. We kind of think of these strengths as superpowers. Go ahead and mark any that you believe apply to you, even if only occasionally. You may not identify with all of them, but you may be able to come up with a few ways that you manifest some of them.

- Appreciation and gratitude (Can you, at least sometimes, appreciate what the world offers?)

- Bravery (Asking for help, even by simply picking up this book, is an example of bravery.)

- Creativity (Creativity can take many forms; for example, from the visual arts to the performing arts to how you approach problems. Be creative in thinking about your own creativity!)

- Curiosity (This doesn't just mean school learning; it can mean learning about music, sports, arts, nature, or even learning about other people.)

- Forgiveness (It's not just for other people. Can you forgive yourself?)

- Hope (This is a tough one with depression. But if you're working on your depression with this book, with a therapist or on your own, you must have some hope inside you.)

- Humility and modesty (These are different from putting yourself down.)

- Humor and playfulness (This can also be hard in depression, but humor can come from dark places.)

- Justice (Do you believe in creating fairness in an unfair world?)

- Kindness (Have you ever offered or received kindness?)

- Leadership (This strength also includes self-leadership.)

- Open-mindedness (Can you be open to new ideas, new people, and new thoughts?)

- Persistence (Sticking with school, therapy, a friendship, or learning something are all examples of persistence. And when you're depressed, just getting yourself out of bed most days is a powerful example of persistence.)

- Perspective and wisdom (Yes, even young people can have perspective and wisdom, especially when they've overcome challenges!)

- Social intelligence (Understanding other people's emotions and having empathy are both examples.)

- Spirituality (As a way of looking at the world, spirituality isn't limited to the formal practice of religion.)

Which of these do you think are your biggest strengths and why?

_____

_____

_____

_____

When in your life have you relied on some of these strengths?

_____

_____

_____

_____

# Acceptance

Anyone who is struggling with a depressed mood would undoubtedly agree that the feelings seem unbearable at times. Research even shows that the impact of a low mood on the brain is similar to what happens in the brain when people are in physical pain. In a word, depression hurts.

We like to talk to our clients about how depression is like a front of bad weather—sometimes very bad—that's moving through. To the person battered by the storm, it may seem that it will never end, that the dark clouds cover everything and clear skies will never return.

Building the muscle of "acceptance" helps in learning to ride out these storms and find the calm spaces—the eye of the storm—within them. These skills can help you be resilient when the dark weather descends.

But be careful here. We aren't saying that you should give up, or suck it up. The trick is to not fight a battle you can't win against your emotions, nor try to control and shove them away when they arrive. Can you fight a rainstorm? No, but you can get a good-quality jacket that fits you and can protect you from the elements. You'll need to take action to help yourself, and while this book can't make you take action, it can help you figure out which actions will be best for you.

We encourage you to recognize, and even feel, the emotional storms for what they are, but instead of fueling them with thoughts from Sgt. Mind, to get busy doing things to cope and go after what's important to you despite the cruddy emotional "weather."

## Try This: Lake Meditation

The following meditation can help you remain calm, like the bottom of a lake. This can be a useful tool as the practice before, during, and after the tougher episodes of stormy emotion common to depression. It can be done in most any position, though you may find it most helpful lying down, perhaps with a cushion beneath you.

Take a moment and bring your attention to the sensations of your body settling into the softness beneath you.

Now imagine a lake. Perhaps this is a place where you have spent time, or maybe you've seen it in pictures. Just imagine the water resting in the earth, the way you are resting in the cushions beneath you.

Consider the surface of the lake, imagining the ways it changes depending on the time of day or the season—still and reflective in the morning as fog lifts off the surface, or perhaps there are some ripples in the afternoon. And though the surface may change, underneath, deep down at the bottom, the water is still.

As the weather changes, the surface may change. Thousands of raindrops may beat down on the surface, or the sun may warm the first few inches, or wind may create waves and small whitecaps on the top of the lake. Yet underneath, there is stillness, farther down toward the bottom.

Seasons change, and in this way the lake's surface changes as well. The reflection one day may be a summer sky and clouds, and then soon golden leaves fall on the surface of the lake, as the trees reflect bright autumn colors in place of summer green. As winter approaches, the surface may reflect the drab surroundings, until finally it freezes over with ice, then snow atop the ice. Even as springtime comes and the ice and snow begin to melt and the sky brightens, through it all the bottom of the lake remains still, resting, calm.

And so while the outside world may change with time and situations that you encounter, these need not disturb the stillness, peace, and quiet underneath. Can you find the stillness deep inside of yourself, allowing yourself to rest there and ease your anxiety and worries?

Take the lake's wisdom and lie down now for the next few minutes with the strength and stillness through whatever arises around you and within you.

## Motivation

When Sgt. Mind is around, it can be extremely hard to have energy to motivate yourself, even to get out of bed and do the basics on a daily basis. With Sgt. Mind holding us back, we then feel even worse about ourselves and more depleted. This is part of the vicious cycle of depression.

## SMART GOALS

Procrastination and lack of motivation can be big problems made worse by depression. There are some good ways to stay motivated with those things you need to get done, and one method is the widely used SMART system for achieving your goals.

SMART goals, whether for homework, dating, or mental health, should be specific, measurable, action oriented, realistic, and time related. Let's imagine you have a big research paper for history coming up.

**S**pecific:

Not: *I'll stop procrastinating.*

Instead: *I'll start taking notes for my paper.*

**M**easurable:

Not: *I'll get my work done for social studies.*

Instead: *I'll take notes on three books.*

**A**ction oriented:

Not: *I'll just write it.*

Instead: *I'll go to the library and get the books I need. Then I'll take notes and after that, I'll make an outline…*

**R**ealistic:

Not: *I'll use fifteen sources, write twenty-five pages, and do an archaeological dig to get artifacts from a Civil War battlefield.*

Instead: *I'll do the best I can in doing the research for this paper.*

**Time related:**

Not: *I'll get the whole paper written in one night—I'm great at winging it.*

Instead: *I'll break this into pieces, doing a bit each day. Today I'll get to the library after school for the books and start taking notes.*

Think of something you're struggling to get motivated with. Write down SMART goals that can help you:

**Specific:** _____

_____

**Measurable:** _____

_____

**Action oriented:** _____

_____

**Realistic:** _____

_____

**Time related:** _____

_____

## THE TIME-LESS MACHINE

You've heard of time machines that take you into the past or future; for now, imagine that you're getting into a time-LESS machine. This contraption doesn't move you back or forward on a timeline, but instead it erases time altogether so that there's only the present moment. It shows you what you do on a daily basis that you find so enjoyable and engaging that you lose track of time.

What would that be like? For Mitch, these time-LESS things include writing, playing with his kids, meditating, working out, and going out to dinner with his wife. For Chris, it's traveling, hiking, cooking, and time with his baby.

Whether you're interacting with people or on your own, at school or at home or elsewhere, when you do these things, time drops away, and you just flow into doing them. Even if you're not overflowing with energy these days, you don't have to be convinced to do these things. And once you're doing them, Sgt. Mind gets quiet, or at least you don't hear him. List a few of these activities here:

_____

_____

_____

_____

## Healthy Choices

We hardly need to tell you that depression is unpleasant—that it feels lousy in our minds as well as in our bodies. To get away from those feelings, it's natural to try to change how we feel through distraction or avoidance. Often these help in the short term, but over time can make things even worse—they are ways of struggling against the quicksand that end up sinking us deeper. And once we get into certain habits—drinking, drugs, cutting, or acting out, for example—they can be very hard to break.

You're probably also aware that there are both healthy and unhealthy ways of coping with your depression. Do you recognize any of these in yourself? Use the blank lines to add others that you've discovered on your own.

| Usually Healthy | Usually Unhealthy | Okay in Moderation |
|---|---|---|
| Cooking | Avoiding social situations | Comfort foods |
| Crafting | Bingeing on junk food | Napping |
| Dancing | Blaming others | Time online, including social media |
| Drawing or painting | Blaming yourself | TV or movies |
| Exercise | Cutting or self-harm | Vegging out |
| Getting into nature | Drinking | Venting your tough feelings to someone |
| Grooming | Drugs | _____ |
| Listening to music | Isolating yourself | _____ |
| Looking at artwork | Skipping activities you care about | |
| Playing music | Skipping class or school | |
| Reading | Smoking | |
| Studying | Taking your feelings out on others, physically or emotionally | |
| Taking a shower or bath | Withdrawing from people | |
| Talking about what bothers you | _____ | |
| Time with friends, family | _____ | |
| Time with your pet | | |
| Volunteering | | |
| Writing | | |
| _____ | | |
| _____ | | |

Which of these are healthy choices you sometimes make?

_____

_____

_____

Which of these are unhealthy choices you sometimes make? If you're at all uncomfortable writing these down, you could make a mental list instead.

_____

_____

_____

Which healthy or moderate choices can you choose to do in the next week?

_____

_____

_____

And now put them in your calendar, or set a reminder to do them!

Most people can relate to a few in each column. This exercise isn't about making you perfect all the time, but trying to find a few more in the healthy column that work for you. By using this book, you can also start to learn which of these will be most helpful for you in which situations.

## Gratitude

Research in positive psychology suggests that people who regularly practice gratitude boost their moods, reduce their anxiety, and are happier with their relationships, not just in the moment but also over time. In a recent study of seven hundred kids aged ten to fourteen, those who were most grateful were

15 percent more satisfied with their lives, and 15 percent less depressed. Their happiness and hopefulness got a significant boost, and they were less likely to get in trouble for cheating, to use substances, or to get sent to detention for their behavior at school.

Mindfulness teacher Thich Nhat Hanh often talks about having a non-toothache. He describes how easy it is to go through life forgetting that we don't have a toothache most of the time, but when we do have a toothache, it can be impossible to forget. So remember, he advises, and enjoy your non-toothache. The larger point is to be aware of not just the positive things we have in life but also to be aware of the absence of negative things.

Gratitude is more than just a feel-good approach. It is a rock-solid strategy for improving mood and well-being, and it offers a direct counter to Sgt. Mind's usual "everything sucks" attitude. To cultivate gratitude in your daily experience, try gratitude journaling.

Using a diary, journal, or regular notebook, spend a few minutes every night before going to bed responding to one or more of the following prompts. At the very least, write a sentence or two where you answer this simple question: what went well today? We suggest actually going a step further. Ask yourself over the course of a longer stretch, what went well this week? Just jot down one or two things from your life for each day. Have a try at a first gratitude journal entry right now. Thinking about today, what went well?

_____

_____

_____

_____

_____

_____

You can also respond to these other prompts:

- Describe a very meaningful experience from the past year. Explain what made it special, and why you're grateful for it.

- Write about a time when someone went out of his or her way for you. How did you feel about it then? How do you feel about it now?

- Write about a special favor you did for someone else. How did you feel about it then? How do you feel about it now?

- What do you appreciate the most about your closest friend?

- What might your closest friend appreciate the most about you?

- What is your favorite thing to do? How does it make you feel, and how would you describe what it means to you?

- What was something that made you smile today (even if just for a moment)?

# Down and Out or Up and In?

In this chapter, we discussed some of the psychological ways depression and Sgt. Mind appear. We've also covered different strategies and activities to change your relationship with your thoughts and feelings.

What have you learned from this chapter about how depression gets you *down* in your mood so that you're checking *out* of daily life?

_____

_____

_____

_____

What specific strategies or ideas from this chapter might help you lift your mood *up* and move you *in* toward people and activities?

_____

_____

_____

_____

What one strategy, idea, or tool are you willing to put to use in the next twenty-four hours? Write it here, and commit to doing so.

_____

_____

_____

# chapter 5

# Social Approaches
# to Depression

A dream you dream alone is only a dream.
A dream you dream together is reality.

—Yoko Ono

Remember Chris's patient from chapter 3? She said that eating and being with people was important medicine that she didn't always like, but she knew if she took it, she would feel better.

In this final chapter, we want to talk about the social side of depression, and the social aspects of getting better—your relationships with other people, and with yourself. Some sections will cover both mindfulness and positive psychology. Other exercises will focus on skills for interacting with people and reaching out and reengaging with the world.

## Reaching Out to Others

For anyone fighting depression, reaching out to other people may be low on your to-do list. Sgt. Mind is quick to tell you that other people—even close friends and family—won't be worth it. This can make it feel next to impossible to drag yourself out to see others, or to even pick up the phone to chat.

But even though Sgt. Mind is trying to keep you safe and protect you from feeling worse, he just doesn't get it. He doesn't see that keeping your social world small also keeps you more depressed. Our brains are built to connect with others—we're social creatures by nature. When we isolate ourselves, it keeps our brains from getting the neurochemical "juice" they need to break free of depression.

List some people in your circle of friends or family who know about your depression and whom you can reach out to in hard times.

_____

_____

_____

_____

_____

List some people who just make you feel better to be around, whether you talk about your depression or not. (Consider friends, teammates, people you're in clubs or activities with, relatives, family friends, teachers, therapists, clergy, and other important mentors.)

_____

_____

_____

List some people who can remind you to use mindfulness and positive-psychology skills in moments when you are stuck, distressed, or overwhelmed.

_____

_____

_____

The people we choose to spend our time with have a tremendous influence on how we view ourselves and the world, and on our behavior. The concept is simple—emotions, like viruses, are contagious. This is bad news if you surround yourself with negative people, but good news if you spend time with positive people.

Who are the five people you spend the most time with?

_____

_____

_____

_____

What kinds of outlook do they have on the world?

_____

_____

_____

_____

How do those people really make you feel? Close your eyes and bring them to mind. As you visualize each of them, notice how you feel in both your body and your mind, and write that down here.

_____

_____

_____

_____

How do you think they influence you and your depression?

_____

_____

_____

_____

When you're positive, people generally want to be around you, but it can be hard to be positive. One challenge we both remember from our teenage years is that many peers find it easier to connect around negative things, like complaining about teachers or putting down lame bands or saying this or that show or game is stupid. Basically, it's a lot easier to complain than it is to take a risk, to be vulnerable and talk about someone or something that you really like. When you're depressed, this can be an especially tempting way to connect with others, but in the long run, you end up surrounded by more negativity.

Sgt. Mind is a born hater, and his way of connecting is around negativity. Misery loves company, but we encourage you to remember to connect more around the positive.

Who can you talk to about what you love, not just what you hate?

_____

_____

_____

_____

Make a list of some of the positive people in your life, including friends, classmates, teammates, relatives, supportive adults like teachers, counselors, and others. You might also include people you aren't close to but want to spend more time with.

_____

_____

_____

_____

_____

Which of these people can you reach out to in the next week?

_____

_____

_____

_____

_____

# Treating Yourself Kindly

It's important to consider not only *who* you're with and how this will affect your mood but also *how* you're treating yourself. Sgt. Mind's voice can be strong, especially in the face of setbacks. He's very fond of blaming you or others, both

107

of which leave you feeling helpless and worse about yourself. But you're not helpless; you do have power to take action even in tough situations. When you're overwhelmed with emotion, it's easy to believe Sgt. Mind and his blame game. In the following exercise, read the example given, and then try correcting Sgt. Mind's negativity in the other scenarios.

Self-blame: *I failed the test because I'm dumb.*

Blaming others: *I failed the test because the teacher is such a…jerk.* (Or maybe you'd use a stronger word here.)

Taking action: *It was a tough test. Maybe I can talk to the teacher or someone else about a different way to study next time.*

Self-blame: *I'll never get a date to the prom because I'm an ugly loser.*

Blaming others: *Everyone at this school is so stuck-up, and the dance is stupid anyway.*

Taking action: _____

_____

Self-blame: *We lost the game because of me.*

Blaming others: *The ref was completely unfair and biased toward the other team.*

Taking action: _____

_____

Self-blame: *I can't pass the driver's test; I'm such an idiot.*

Blaming others: *I don't want my license anyway, and the examiner is such a jerk.*

Taking action: _____

_____

Self-blame: *I always procrastinate. Now I have ten pages to write by tomorrow morning!*

Blaming others: *My stupid teacher kept me late at school, and my mom wants me to finish the dishes.*

Taking action: _____

_____

Self-blame: *My depression is keeping me from working and socializing.*

Blaming others: *Other people are holding me back and making me depressed.*

Taking action: _____

_____

Sgt. Mind's voice can be pretty nasty. He'll hide evidence that doesn't prove his point, and show you only one side of things. And he makes you feel like what he says is true. We're going to suggest something that might seem very strange at first—to take a moment and listen to him, but also listen to your own true voice, your compassionate voice.

## Try This: Talking to Yourself Compassionately

Find a comfortable and sustainable posture, and close your eyes. Now bring to mind a recent moment when Sgt. Mind was really laying into you. It could be just a small thing, like something you wish you hadn't said or done, but he took you to task. Or think about some quality about yourself that you aren't crazy about: *I need to be more assertive*; *I eat too much*; *I stall about doing my homework too often.*

If this is painful, you might just want to notice that. You could say to yourself, *Wow, this hurts*, or use other words that work for you.

What is the purpose of the voice? Is it trying to help in some way, under the hurt and suffering? Does it want anything good, even if the way it tries to help is not helpful? If you can notice that, maybe just thank the voice. If you can't, just continue to label the pain, but maybe also place a hand or two over your heart.

Sometimes Sgt. Mind can quiet down or step aside, but not always. If he does step aside, see if you can hear another, more compassionate voice. Sometimes it doesn't even sound like a voice but is just a warm sensation. What words does this voice want to share with you? They might be words you would share with a suffering friend: *You're okay in spite of mistakes* or *You will be stronger for this in the long run* or other words that feel best.

Notice again how your mind and body feel.

You can even do a short version of this self-compassion practice by checking in with yourself mindfully every so often, like the middle part of this practice, and then asking yourself, *What else is here?* It's important to notice not just the lousy feelings and thoughts but also what else might be present.

So go ahead right now, be still, take a breath, and ask yourself, *Besides the depression, besides Sgt. Mind, what else is here?*

## Try This: Kind Wishes Practice

It can often be hard to feel like we deserve any good things coming our way, especially when we're depressed. But we can feel better only if we start to want to feel better. We aren't suggesting empty affirmations like "I'm happy" or "I'm safe," especially if you don't believe them. But maybe you can make these wishes for yourself: *May I be happy* or *May I be safe*. Research has shown that making the wish works and actually helps you feel better, while those empty affirmations can actually make you feel worse.

When we make kind wishes for ourselves, we build the muscle of self-compassion, making the compassionate voice more likely than Sgt. Mind to come up with the answer. But sometimes it's hard to make kind wishes for ourselves; it might help to start with someone else who feels easier. When we make kind wishes for others, we open our hearts and in the process feel better.

Try making some kind wishes, and see how you feel before, during, and after. You can write these down in a journal or somewhere else, or just do them in your head every so often. Start with an easy one:

- What is a wish you have for someone you care about?

- What is a wish someone who cares about you might have for you? (It could be a friend, a family member, even a therapist or another adult.)

- What is a wish you have for yourself?

And now see how it feels to make some wishes for other people in the world:

- Make a wish for someone you don't know very well.

- Make a wish for someone who gets under your skin.

How hard was this? What do you think that might mean? And how do you feel after doing this exercise?

# Social Media

More and more, teens and adults live their social lives online. It can be wonderful to stay connected with friends and acquaintances anytime we want, but it can also be overwhelming to feel like we are constantly comparing. In the authors' day, it used to be that you had to look good and act a certain way during the school day. Now many young people feel they have to look good and act a certain way all the time, online and off. That's a lot of work and worry. We hear firsthand from kids (and have experienced ourselves) the stress of navigating social media. And while there is research to suggest that spending time on social media sinks your self-esteem, we aren't going to tell you to stay away. But we are going to suggest you approach it wisely and mindfully.

One interesting piece of research that doesn't get talked about much is that while looking at other people's social media often makes people feel worse or inadequate about themselves, looking at your own social media can actually make you feel better. That's because when we compare our insides to other people's outsides, we generally feel worse. So next time you're on social media, take some time to read over your own feed, look at your own pictures, and don't think about anyone else. See how doing so makes you feel.

Take a deep breath (maybe the 7-11 breath you read about in chapter 2), and allow your thoughts to settle. Now grab your phone or tablet or computer, and hold it in your hand. Notice how it feels just to hold. Take a moment to click on the icon and look over your social media. Go ahead and open up your favorites.

Without looking at anyone else's (hard, right?), just click over and look at your own profile and updates for a few minutes.

What kinds of things do you notice?

_____

_____

_____

_____

How do you feel after doing this?

_____

_____

_____

# Be the Change

Mahatma Gandhi once said, "Be the change you wish to see in the world." With that in mind, some of the strongest research in positive psychology points to helping others as one of the best ways to boost your mood. When we help others, we feel better about ourselves. We feel like we matter and can make a difference in the world. One of the worst parts of depression is feeling like you don't matter. But you do.

A lot of teens find it hard to get started with community service, not knowing where to start, or not feeling like they have anything to offer in helping others. Go online or talk to some adults; maybe your school or spiritual community has a service coordinator, or your parents or their friends (or even your friends' parents) have ideas or opportunities for you. It doesn't have to be boring; you can share your passions and talents with others who will appreciate them, and who knows, you might make new friends or end up with an actual job in the process!

Here are several suggestions to get you started:

Do you love the outdoors? Are you a beach bum?

*Organize a beach or park cleanup, on your own or with friends.*

Do you like people and have creative talents but lack an audience?

*Work with the elderly or handicapped. Sing for them, tell them stories, show them your artwork, or teach them computer skills.*

Love food? Love cooking?

*Help out by cooking or bringing food and ingredients to a homeless shelter or delivering meals to people who have a hard time getting out.*

Are you a talented visual artist?

*See about creating a mural somewhere in your town or putting on an art exhibition at a local coffee shop, community center, or senior center.*

Good at school, or even just good enough? Enjoy time with kids?

*Tutor or mentor younger kids after school. Many schools and organizations have opportunities for this.*

Are there local or global issues that matter to you?

*Volunteer for a public awareness campaign about an important political or social issue.*

Love sports, enjoy kids?

*Find out about becoming an assistant coach or referee of a youth league.*

Dog person? Cat person? Animal lover?

*Volunteer your time helping out at an animal shelter.*

Like quiet spaces and access to free books and movies?

*Ask for some hours helping at the local library.*

Fashionista?

*Organize a clothing drive for folks in need with friends, or gather stuff you no longer wear. It can feel great to free up room in your closet.*

Enjoy big groups, and maybe even telling people what to do?

*Join or help organize a day of service with your school, youth group, or another organization you belong to.*

Care about depression and mental health issues?

*Get involved with an advocacy organization for young people struggling with depression and other issues, or consider working for a hotline if you're old enough.*

Like this book?

*Teach someone mindfulness!*

Any other ideas you can think of? Write them here:

_____

_____

_____

_____

_____

# Positive Planning

A significant portion of depression involves withdrawing, avoiding, or in some way not doing things to make yourself feel better. Again, as we said at the start of this book—depression sucks. And it sucks away your desire to go after pleasurable things. By this point in the book, you've hopefully seen that doing some of our recommended activities and strategies, rather than listening to Sgt. Mind, helps your feelings change. Here, we're going to look at how you can ignore Sgt. Mind's orders, and choose to do specific things to start sparking positive feelings.

Don't be surprised if fireworks don't light up the sky when you first start. Feelings will change, but that can take time, so hang in there!

## Feel-Better Bingo

Here's a bingo game for you to play right now or later, with a friend. You can download additional copies at http://www.newharbinger.com/33827; see the back of the book for instructions.

The rules are simple. You win by looking at the card below and selecting at least five squares or positive activities to do. Using your Feelings Thermometer from chapter 4, keep track of how your mood changes by measuring how you're feeling before and after these activities. The trick will be to see if you can come up with five so that you score a BINGO on the card. If you're up for a challenge, try banging out a BINGO before a friend can, or see if you can get all five in on a single day. We're sure you get the point here—just get yourself moving, doing, and engaging in stuff and notice how you feel. See if Sgt. Mind was right after all.

| B | I | N | G | O |
|---|---|---|---|---|
| Listen to music | Look at fun, old pictures | Exercise | Walk in nature | Do something helpful for someone |
| Read something for fun and tell someone about it | Play a board/video game with someone | Take a hot bath | Get a massage | Hang out at a coffee shop |
| Call or text a friend | Eat a favorite dessert or cook something yummy | FREE (Just be mindful for a while) | Write a thank-you letter or e-mail | See a cool movie |
| Get a new outfit | Do something creative | Fix something | Smell something sweet or soothing | Walk five laps around the inside of a mall |
| Tell a joke or listen to comedy | Dig out your favorite old toy | Play a fun practical joke on someone | Tell the story of a big event from the past | Watch a favorite show |

What did you notice about your mood before doing these activities?

_____

_____

_____

_____

How do you feel after doing this? What happened to Sgt. Mind?

_____

_____

_____

_____

# Your Drop-in-the-Bucket List

Now that you've hopefully shifted your mood a bit toward the positive, see if you're willing to go a step further. This word search, which can also be downloaded at http://www.newharbinger.com/33827, includes a number of possible bucket-list items many people might select as things they'd like to do at some point in life. With depression, sometimes it can be hard to allow yourself to think, plan, and want into the future, but learning to do so is an important skill all by itself. Take some time now and have fun finding and circling bucket-list items that appeal to you. (The answers are in a key at the end of the book.)

| A | D | H | Z | X | D | O | L | P | H | I | N | S | S | U | R | F | I | N | G |
| B | Y | C | I | T | R | U | E | L | O | V | E | S | D | D | W | R | Y | L | F |
| U | E | R | S | T | E | E | I | G | T | S | E | R | O | F | N | I | A | R | W |
| C | R | U | E | T | A | G | I | V | A | N | M | U | C | R | I | C | L | Z | F |
| S | A | I | V | H | M | L | E | H | I | U | R | O | T | N | E | M | P | H | L |
| L | U | S | I | Q | C | G | Y | S | R | G | G | B | O | B | C | A | N | A | A |
| W | Q | E | D | M | A | R | U | M | B | A | U | N | R | O | N | U | E | N | S |
| O | S | I | Y | S | R | B | A | L | A | L | E | M | A | C | O | T | E | G | H |
| B | S | N | K | T | A | N | O | E | L | C | W | S | T | L | Y | H | R | G | M |
| R | E | D | S | T | A | U | L | R | L | A | T | U | E | V | N | O | C | L | O |
| E | M | I | R | T | V | S | I | P | O | T | T | E | R | Y | A | R | S | I | B |
| P | I | A | E | R | I | D | E | H | O | R | S | E | B | A | C | K | A | D | M |
| U | T | E | E | A | E | I | D | C | N | A | O | A | E | L | D | F | B | E | I |
| S | S | J | T | L | U | M | O | Z | Z | Z | E | F | C | P | N | O | B | V | L |
| G | R | U | N | A | M | A | R | A | T | H | O | N | O | A | A | N | E | E | C |
| N | Y | G | U | I | S | R | S | A | I | L | I | N | G | N | R | D | Y | R | K |
| I | K | G | L | T | J | Y | A | W | D | A | O | R | B | I | G | U | R | E | C |
| I | W | L | O | R | B | P | A | I | N | T | E | B | I | T | L | E | O | S | O |
| K | R | E | V | A | S | E | F | I | L | V | E | N | I | C | E | O | A | T | R |
| S | C | I | P | M | Y | L | O | E | S | U | O | H | M | A | E | R | D | T | D |

What items did you come up with? List at least the top five:

1. _____

2. _____

3. _____

4. _____

5. _____

Now imagine yourself actually doing any or all of these at some point in the future. What do you notice yourself thinking and feeling?

_____

_____

_____

_____

_____

What does Sgt. Mind have to say about it?

_____

_____

_____

Based on all you've learned so far in the book about managing tough emotions and thoughts, how might you respond to him?

Here's why this is a drop-in-the-bucket list: you have to start somewhere. An empty bucket left outside fills up with rainwater one drop at a time. What is something you're willing to do at this moment that moves you in the direction of a bucket-list item? Are you willing to commit to doing that first step, and if so, how does it feel to make that choice?

Who can you share your bucket-list items with? Who can support you in taking the steps toward making some of these cool things a reality?

# Motivate Yourself to Be Positive

For many people, struggling with depression can feel like an uphill battle—like they're up against something with an incredible amount of momentum behind it. Mitch's grandfather was fond of witty and mildly wise sayings, and one of these applies to this sense of momentum. He used to say that "some things are hard to stop—sort of like trying to stop a lava flow by spitting on it." And that's the way it can seem with depression—too much lava-like momentum. Thankfully, this book gives you ways to get on top of depression that are much more effective than spitting on lava!

Imagine spending an entire day on a field trip to a museum paired up with a guy like Drabner. On the bus ride, Drabner sits slouched and doesn't seem to care that his messy backpack is open and used candy wrappers and unnamed bits of crud are spilling out onto your own bag. He doesn't make eye contact with you at all, and if you ask him anything, he either mumbles "I dunno," or doesn't answer at all. His clothes are wrinkled and a bit dirty. He makes annoyed faces and sighs whenever anyone expresses any enthusiasm or seems to be having a decent time.

Ask yourself: How would you honestly feel after an entire day with Drabner? If you were able to pick a partner for the next class trip, would you choose him?

When people present a gloomy exterior to the world, it can be contagious to everyone else, and guess what—they end up even more isolated and feeling even worse. Even though the momentum toward the negative is strong, and even though Sgt. Mind may be telling you to give up, a big part of breaking out of depressive patterns of emotion and behavior is to practice positivity, especially when you don't feel like it.

You've probably heard the saying "Fake it till you make it." We're not suggesting that you walk around faking happiness all the time; people will be able to tell, and you'll feel worse. What we are saying is that you have the power to choose to do anything despite what Sgt. Mind says.

One surprising piece of research shows that motivation often comes after, not before, a behavior. Basically, sometimes you need to simply start doing something before you'll feel like doing it more, whether it's working out, talking to new people, or doing a depression workbook. So how can you practice positivity in the face of a depressive lack of motivation?

## Try This: Do Yourself a FAVOR

Practice on your own first, right now, mindfully becoming aware of what it feels like to go through each of the steps.

- **F**ace open and expressive—This includes making eye contact with people and making sure you have a pleasant, or at least not distressed or irritable, expression.

- **A**lert and upright posture—Sitting up sends a signal to yourself and to others of being engaged, interested, confident, and receptive.

- **V**oice positive and pleasant—Here, you're not being fake; you're talking in an interested, "into it" way because you want to make a good impression.

- **O**ptimistic talk—This means letting Sgt. Mind's negative views pass by without immediately grabbing them and sharing them with others.

- **R**esponsiveness—Here's where you don't let the ball drop when others make comments, ask something of you, or in some way send a signal that they'd like a response from you.

Putting your best foot forward is not always easy, especially when Sgt. Mind is chattering loudly, or when your emotions are dark and unpredictable. But these skills can be practiced and developed despite what's happening internally for you. Try it and see for yourself. Here are some suggestions for practice:

- Try on these FAVOR behaviors in front of a mirror. Notice how Sgt. Mind might be running wild internally with judgment and ridicule, but keep moving forward, putting on these behaviors as if they were new clothes.

- Select a support person from your network and try a role-play. First be your typical self, then try being Drabner, and then do yourself with the FAVOR behaviors. Ask for honest feedback about each role, and discuss what it was like interacting with the different characters.

- Write down some ways that you present yourself in a best-foot-forward way (like when you volunteer for something hard, or help someone out when you don't need to). Choose one or more of these behaviors to consciously replace with FAVOR behaviors for a particular day. Spend the day trying out these replacement behaviors and observe any differences in how people respond, even if they are small. This step is crucial—you're likely missing the positive feedback and signals others have been sending you because you've been buying into Sgt. Mind's dark, negative opinions about yourself. If you make a point of looking for the actual evidence in people's responses, you may be pleasantly surprised.

- Assume a FAVOR attitude and approach everyone—teachers, cafeteria staff, cashiers, salespeople, coaches, and others—from this positive standpoint. You might feel different, and people might respond to you differently. The key is not to fake positivity, but to share your best you, the you that's already there.

Describe any evidence of people's responses to FAVOR behaviors, or your skillful responses to Sgt. Mind's protests against your practice efforts.

_____

_____

_____

_____

_____

# Interpersonal Power: Assertiveness and Effectiveness

Assertiveness is basically the skill of speaking up for yourself and going after what matters to you, in an honest, respectful, and straightforward way.

Here's a short list of its benefits:

- Earns others' respect

- Makes it more likely you'll get things you want

- Helps you avoid sticky, potentially hurtful situations

- Can help prevent tough situations from getting worse

- Draws in others to you

- Builds self-confidence and self-respect

With his dark, depressive glasses, Sgt. Mind likes to tell you to either back away from challenging situations (be passive) or push too hard (be aggressive). He can make it hard to hit the sweet spot of assertiveness, but these tips can help you learn to be more assertive:

- Use mindfulness. Catch yourself saying things like "I don't know" or "I don't care" or "Whatever you think," and try replacing them with "I think" or "I'd prefer" or "I don't know right now, but give me a moment to consider."

- When you're asking for something, stand up straight, make eye contact, and use a clear, direct, polite voice.

- Practice in settings where the interactions are less personal; for example, with store clerks, support people on the phone, or servers in restaurants.

- To let people know what you think and feel, start with "I feel…" or "I think it's important that…"

- Watch people who are good at being assertive. How do they talk, walk, and act? Try to model some of your behaviors on theirs.

- If you have a habit of interrupting people, apologize ("Oh, I'm sorry I cut you off...") and let them have their say. Notice their reactions to this.

- Ask others' opinions and listen fully to them. Notice how they seem to respond to you.

- Never put down others for their thoughts or opinions. Tell them you can agree to disagree, or simply say, "I guess we see it differently."

Part of staying positive and keeping Sgt. Mind and depression at bay is using strategies like those in this chapter to build positive relationships with yourself and others. We know that a lot of this book is about action, and action is hard when you're depressed. But it's hard to think your way into a new way of feeling. Sometimes you have to get out there and act your way into the new life that you want for yourself.

# Down and Out or Up and In?

This chapter was about making choices around the people and actions that will bring more positivity into your life, and reset the cycle of negativity and depression. Making friends and keeping them doesn't happen without both sides working hard, and getting out of unhealthy relationships is also not easy. But you may have discovered that you're a lot less alone than you think, and that can be a good enough reason to keep putting in effort even when Sgt. Mind is suggesting otherwise.

What have you learned from this chapter about how depression gets you *down* in your mood so that you're checking *out* of daily life?

_____

_____

_____

_____

What specific strategies or ideas from this chapter might help you lift your mood *up* and move you *in* toward people and activities?

_____

_____

_____

_____

What one strategy, idea, or tool are you willing to put to use in the next twenty-four hours? Write it here, and commit to doing so.

_____

_____

_____

# Conclusion

If you're reading this (and hopefully you're not the type who just skipped to the end!), you've come quite a long way from where you started. You've learned a number of skills, strategies, and approaches for dealing with depression (and sidestepping Sgt. Mind). You've developed tools for all the main areas of your life—your physical, mental, and social functioning. It's our wish that you've not just learned some mindfulness and positive psychology skills, but that—more importantly—you've also learned to trust your own capacity to connect with the moments of your life, relate to them flexibly, and act with creativity and purpose. It's this core of your own choice and power that really makes the difference in your moving beyond depression and into the good things ahead of you in life.

It's been our privilege to serve as your guides on this journey. As this trip comes to an end, and before you begin your next one, we'd like to suggest one final practice. This is one to keep and to carry with you. Bring it out whenever you need a reminder of all you've learned in this book. Use it whenever you need a healthy jolt of mindfulness.

## Try This: Inward, Upward, and Outward

For this final practice, sit comfortably and close your eyes. Breathe easily and normally. After taking a minute or two to settle, repeat the following slowly and silently to yourself.

"May I…

Treat my body with care…

Hold my thoughts lightly…

Ride out the emotional storms…

Reach out toward others…

So that I know…

Peace…

Power…

and happiness…

And may all those who suffer know the same."

In all that you do, we wish you peace and happiness.

—Chris and Mitch

# Answers

## (to the activity Your Drop-in-the-Bucket list)

**KEY:** ABBEYROAD / ACTINAPLAY / ALCATRAZ / ARCHERY / AUTHOR / BROADWAY / BULLRIDE / CAMEL / CIRCUMNAVIGATE / COASTTOCOAST / CRUISE / DOCTORATE / DOLPHINS / DREAMCAR / DREAMHOUSE / EVEREST / FLASHMOB / FLY / FONDUE / GRANDCANYON / HANGGLIDE / HOTAIRBALLOON / INDIA / ITALY / JUGGLE / LEARNLANGUAGE / LIFESAVER / LOUVRE / MANATEES / MARTIALART / MENTOR / OLYMPICS / PAINT / POTTERY / PYRAMIDS / RAINFOREST / RIDEHORSEBACK / ROCKCLIMB / RUNAMARATHON / SAILING / SCREENPLAY / SCUBA / SKIING / SKYDIVE /STARTABUSINESS / SUPERBOWL / SURFING / TIBET/ TIMESSQUARE / TOURACASTLE / TRUELOVE / VEGAS / VENICE / VOLUNTEER

# Acknowledgments

In any book project, there are so many people behind the scenes helping to make it happen, so many people deserving of thanks. We have an immense sense of gratitude to all those we would refer to as teachers and mentors—whether we've known them personally or from a distance—who led us toward the knowledge and drive to write this book. We're very thankful for the teachings of individuals such as Thich Nhat Hanh, His Holiness the XIV Dalai Lama, Chögyam Trungpa Rinpoche, Ram Dass, and Pema Chödrön; Martin Seligman and Christopher Peterson (whose work inspired our list of superpowers); Jon Kabat-Zinn (whose work inspired the Lake Meditation); Doreen Virtue (whose *Constant Craving A–Z* was the basis for the chart on healthy and emotional eating); Steven Hayes, Kirk Strosahl, and Kelly Wilson (whose work inspired the metaphor in chapter 1's visualization exercise and the strategy "say say say" in chapter 4); Susan M. Orsillo and Lizabeth Roemer (for leading us to the practice described by our "floating leaves in a moving stream" meditation); and Joseph Goldstein, Jack Kornfield, Chris Germer, Elisha Goldstein (whose work with Bob Stahl in MBSR popularized the STOP technique), Amy Saltzman, Susan Greenland, and Rupert Spira, among others.

We're thankful as well for colleagues such as those at Manville School / Judge Baker Children's Center, Dr. Donald ("Sandy") Kerr, and members of the Institute for Meditation and Psychotherapy and the Mindfulness in Education Network, all of whom inspired and supported our work on this project. A special thanks to Dzung Vo and Mark Bertin, who reviewed early chapters and offered helpful feedback, and Ashley Sitkin, who advised on the yoga practices.

To Jess O'Brien and Nicola Skidmore (our editors), and certainly many others at New Harbinger Publications, and to Karen Schader (our copyeditor). Your support, thoughtfulness, and guidance clearly resonate in these pages. It's been an amazing experience to work closely with you.

We'd also like to express our thanks to our families. To our wives for supporting us as we departed home for our numerous coffee shop writing sessions, and for giving us the encouragement to follow our creative dharma paths. To our children for making it matter that we do the work of writing for impact out into the world.

And to our clients. You deserve more than our thanks. You deserve the energy of our compassionate awareness now and always.

**Mitch R. Abblett, PhD**, is a clinical psychologist and clinical director of the Manville School, a therapeutic day school program in Boston, MA, serving children and adolescents with emotional, behavioral, and learning difficulties. He maintains a private practice, and has written regarding mindfulness, clinical work, and youth mental health needs. He conducts national and international trainings on mindfulness and its applications.

**Christopher Willard, PsyD**, is a psychologist and educational consultant based in Boston, MA, specializing in mindfulness. He has been practicing meditation for over fifteen years, and leads workshops internationally on the topic of mindfulness for treating young people. He currently serves on the board of directors at the Institute for Meditation and Psychotherapy, and the Mindfulness in Education Network. His thoughts on mental health have been featured in *The New York Times*, on cnn.com, and elsewhere. Willard is author of *Child's Mind, Growing Up Mindful,* and three other books. He teaches on the faculty of Harvard Medical School.

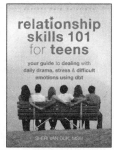

Register your **new harbinger** titles for additional benefits!

When you register your **new harbinger** title—purchased in any format, from any source—you get access to benefits like the following:

- Downloadable accessories like printable worksheets and extra content

- Instructional videos and audio files

- Information about updates, corrections, and new editions

Not every title has accessories, but we're adding new material all the time.

Access free accessories in 3 easy steps:

**1.** Sign in at NewHarbinger.com (or **register** to create an account).

**2.** Click on **register a book**. Search for your title and click the **register** button when it appears.

**3.** Click on the **book cover or title** to go to its details page. Click on **accessories** to view and access files.

That's all there is to it!

If you need help, visit:

NewHarbinger.com/accessories

**new harbinger**
CELEBRATING
**40** YEARS